—

simply*fresh*

whole-food recipes for your Vitamix® 7500™

LIVE
simply*fresh*

With its powerful performance and ultra-responsive controls, the Vitamix® 7500™ will completely change your perception of what a blender can do. Easily create healthy, delicious meals from fresh, whole-food ingredients, and discover why Vitamix is the most trusted brand among professional chefs.

The quality and versatility of your Vitamix 7500 will help you create every possible texture, from chunky nut butters to silky-smooth purées, while it replaces several other kitchen tools. With a Vitamix machine, you can chop, cream, blend, heat, grind, churn, emulsify, crush, whisk, frappé, purée, powder, and whip through every course of every meal.

Enjoy this collection of recipes, specially developed for the Vitamix 7500, and then begin to explore your own creative inventions. Visit us along your culinary journey at vitamix.com for more recipes and inspiration.

every meal, every day

Simply Fresh brings you hundreds of recipes for meals, snacks, and beverages for every day of the week. We want to help you enjoy your Vitamix machine to its fullest potential. In addition to basic recipe notes, you'll find creative tips throughout the book to help you with fun family meals, weekend entertaining, gifts from your kitchen, and much more.

Browse the Beverages section for everything from breakfast smoothies to weekend cocktails. Beyond soups and sauces, Mains shows you dinner entrées you can easily prepare throughout the week. To complete your meals, Desserts brings you frozen sorbets, warm fondues, and other delights like Raisin Almond Cheesecake and Low-Fat Pumpkin Pie. It's all here—simple, delicious recipes to help you plan for every course of every meal.

Simply Fresh is all about maximizing the power of your Vitamix 7500 to help you save time and create exquisite meals to enjoy with family and friends. With Vitamix, every meal is easier, healthier, and more delicious!

beverages

beverages

cocktails • coffees • juice • milks • milkshakes • smoothies

blackberry pear *smoothie*

preparation: 10 minutes • ***processing:*** 30 seconds • ***yield:*** 4 3/4 cups (1.1 l) (4 servings)

1 cup (245 g) low-fat plain yogurt

2/3 cup (160 ml) water

2 bananas, peeled

1 ripe pear, 7 ounces (200 g), halved, cored

2 cups (280 g) frozen blackberries

1. Place all ingredients into the Vitamix container in the order listed and secure lid.

2. Select Variable 1.

3. Switch machine to Start and slowly increase speed to Variable 10.

4. Blend for 30 seconds using the tamper to press the ingredients into the blades.

nutritional information: *Amount Per Serving: Calories 140, Total Fat 2g, Saturated Fat 0.5g, Cholesterol 5mg, Sodium 25mg, Total Carbohydrate 31g, Dietary Fiber 6g, Protein 3g*

green pick
me up *smoothie*

preparation: 10 minutes • **processing:** 30 seconds
yield: 2 1/2 cups (600 ml) (2 servings)

1/2 cup (75 g) green grapes

1/2 orange, peeled

1/2 apple, seeded

2 cups (72 g) Swiss chard

2 cups (480 ml) ice cubes

1. Place all ingredients into the Vitamix container in the order listed and secure lid.

2. Select Variable 1.

3. Switch machine to Start and slowly increase speed to Variable 10.

4. Blend for 30 seconds, using the tamper if needed.

 nutritional information: *Amount Per Serving:
Calories 70, Total Fat 0g, Saturated Fat 0g,
Cholesterol 0mg, Sodium 85mg,
Total Carbohydrate 18g, Dietary Fiber 3g,
Protein 1g*

fun pops for kids

Smoothies can easily be turned into delicious frozen pops, providing another fun way for kids to enjoy their fruits, veggies, and greens. Pour any prepared smoothie into ice pop molds (small paper cups will also work) and freeze until almost solid. Insert wooden craft sticks into each pop so the sticks stand straight. Return to the freezer until completely solid. To remove pops, run a little warm water over the bottom to loosen it from the mold. Play with texture by adding a few fresh berries, or layer two to three different smoothies in the mold for fun color and flavor variety.

pomegranate berry *smoothie*

preparation: 10 minutes • **processing:** 45 seconds • **yield:** 3 3/4 cups (900 ml) (3 servings)

1/2 cup (120 ml) water

1/2 cup (113 g) low-fat cottage cheese

1 cup (240 ml) pomegranate juice

1/2 banana, peeled

2 cups (280 g) frozen mixed berries

1. Place all ingredients into the Vitamix container in the order listed and secure lid.

2. Select Variable 1.

3. Switch machine to Start and slowly increase speed to Variable 10.

4. Blend for 45 seconds.

> **nutritional information:** *Amount Per Serving: Calories 140, Total Fat 1.5g, Saturated Fat 0g, Cholesterol 5mg, Sodium 135mg, Total Carbohydrate 29g, Dietary Fiber 3g, Protein 6g*

summer
blush *smoothie*

preparation: 10 minutes • **processing:** 45 seconds
yield: 4 1/4 cups (1.0 l) (4 servings)

3/4 cup (120 ml) water

2 1/2 cups (375 g) grapes

2 Tablespoons (30 ml) agave nectar
or honey (optional)

2 cups (300 g) frozen unsweetened peach slices

1 cup (150 g) frozen unsweetened raspberries

1. Place all ingredients into the Vitamix container in the order listed and secure lid.

2. Select Variable 1.

3. Switch machine to Start and slowly increase speed to Variable 10, using tamper as needed.

4. Blend for 45 seconds using the tamper to press the ingredients into the blades.

nutritional information: *Amount Per Serving: Calories 90, Total Fat 0g, Saturated Fat 0g, Cholesterol 0mg, Sodium 0mg, Total Carbohydrate 24g, Dietary Fiber 3g, Protein 1g*

---

stock your freezer

Freezing fresh fruit throughout the summer months can be a great cost-saver through the winter. To prevent fresh fruit from becoming a solid frozen block, spread berries or fruit slices in a thin layer on a cookie sheet. Allow to freeze before transferring to a sealable plastic bag.

peach cobbler *smoothie*

preparation: 10 minutes • ***processing:*** 40–45 seconds • ***yield:*** 4 1/2 cups (1.0 l) (4 servings)

3/4 cup (180 g) peach nectar

2 cups (480 g) low-fat vanilla yogurt

1 teaspoon vanilla extract

1 teaspoon honey

1/2 teaspoon ground nutmeg

2 teaspoons wheat germ

4 teaspoons rolled oats

2 cups (372 g) frozen unsweetened peach slices

1 cup (240 ml) ice cubes

1. Place all ingredients into the Vitamix container in the order listed and secure lid.

2. Select Variable 1.

3. Switch machine to Start and slowly increase speed to Variable 10.

4. Blend for 40 to 45 seconds using the tamper to press the ingredients into the blades.

>> **nutritional information:** *Amount Per Serving: Calories 160, Total Fat 1.5g, Saturated Fat 1g, Cholesterol 5mg, Sodium 75mg, Total Carbohydrate 30g, Dietary Fiber 2g, Protein 6g*

note: Soften peaches 15 minutes.

lime and mint *agua fresca*

preparation: 15 minutes • **processing:** 20–30 seconds • **yield:** 2 3/4 cups (660 ml) (2 servings)

1 1/2 cups (360 ml) water

1 Tablespoon agave nectar

1 3/4 cups (298 g) honeydew chunks

1 1/2 cups (200 g) cucumber, peeled, cut into large chunks

1/2 lime, peeled

2 Tablespoons (11 g) fresh spearmint leaves

1/2 teaspoon lime zest

1 cup (240 ml) ice cubes

1. Place all ingredients into the Vitamix container in the order listed and secure lid.

2. Select Variable 1.

3. Switch machine to Start and slowly increase speed to Variable 10.

4. Blend for 20 to 30 seconds using the tamper to press the ingredients into the blades.

>> **nutritional information:** *Amount Per Serving: Calories 70, Total Fat 0g, Saturated Fat 0g, Cholesterol 0mg, Sodium 30mg, Total Carbohydrate 17g, Dietary Fiber 2g, Protein 1g*

note: Garnish with mint sprigs.

tropical sailing *smoothie*

preparation: 10 minutes • **processing:** 20–30 seconds • **yield:** 3 3/4 cups (900 ml) (3 servings)

1 cup (240 ml) orange juice

1 cup (240 g) low-fat vanilla yogurt

1 banana, peeled

1 1/3 cups (250 g) frozen unsweetened pineapple chunks

1. Place all ingredients into the Vitamix container in the order listed and secure lid.

2. Select Variable 1.

3. Switch machine to Start and slowly increase speed to Variable 10, using tamper if needed.

4. Blend for 20 to 30 seconds.

nutritional information: *Amount Per Serving: Calories 190, Total Fat 1.5g, Saturated Fat 0.5g, Cholesterol 5mg, Sodium 55mg, Total Carbohydrate 40g, Dietary Fiber 2g, Protein 6g*

note: To reduce the sweetness of this recipe, use plain or Greek yogurt instead of vanilla.

frosty fruit
refresher *smoothie*

preparation: 10 minutes • **processing:** 25–30 seconds
yield: 4 cups (960 ml) (4 servings)

1 cup (240 ml) 1% milk

8 ounce (227 g) can crushed pineapple, not drained

2 cups (300 g) orange sherbet

1 cup (140 g) frozen unsweetened strawberries

1. Place all ingredients into the Vitamix container in the order listed and secure lid.

2. Select Variable 1.

3. Switch machine to Start and slowly increase speed to Variable 10.

4. Blend for 25 to 30 seconds, using the tamper to press the ingredients into the blades.

 **nutritional information:** *Amount Per Serving: Calories 160, Total Fat 2g, Saturated Fat 1g, Cholesterol 5mg, Sodium 60mg, Total Carbohydrate 33g, Dietary Fiber 2g, Protein 3g*

birthday party refreshment

Instead of sugary punches and sodas at your child's next celebration, try this fresh fruit smoothie. With crushed pineapple, orange sherbet, and frozen strawberries, it has all the citrus zing and bright color of a punch, without the unnecessary calories. Kids will love it served in their favorite cups with a fresh pineapple wedge or strawberry garnish.

garden green *smoothie*

preparation: 20 minutes • **processing:** 40 seconds • **yield:** 4 1/4 cups (1.0 l) (4 servings)

1/4 cup (60 ml) water

1 cup (150 g) green grapes

1 orange, 4 1/2 ounces (128 g),
peeled, halved

1/2 celery stalk, 1 ounce (28 g), halved

1/2 small carrot, 1 ounce (28 g), halved

1 green apple, 6 1/2 ounces (185 g),
cored, quartered

1/2 medium zucchini, 3 1/2 ounces (100 g),
cut into large chunks

1 cup (50 g) romaine lettuce

1 cup (67 g) kale, spine removed

1/2 cup (30 g) parsley leaves

2 cups (480 ml) ice cubes

1. Place all ingredients into the Vitamix container in the order listed and secure lid.

2. Select Variable 1.

3. Switch machine to Start and slowly increase speed to Variable 10.

4. Blend for 40 seconds using the tamper to press the ingredients into the blades.

>> **nutritional information:** *Amount Per Serving: Calories 80, Total Fat 0g, Saturated Fat 0g, Cholesterol 0mg, Sodium 25mg, Total Carbohydrate 19g, Dietary Fiber 3g, Protein 2g*

spicy monkey *smoothie*

preparation: 10 minutes • **processing:** 20–30 seconds • **yield:** 4 cups (960 ml) (4 servings)

2 cups (490 g) low-fat plain yogurt

2 ripe bananas, peeled, halved

1/2 teaspoon ground cinnamon

1/8 teaspoon ground allspice

1/8 teaspoon ground nutmeg

1 cup (240 ml) ice cubes

1. Place all ingredients into the Vitamix container in the order listed and secure lid.

2. Select Variable 1.

3. Switch machine to Start and slowly increase speed to Variable 10.

4. Blend for 20 to 30 seconds.

>> **nutritional information:** *Amount Per Serving: Calories 130, Total Fat 2g, Saturated Fat 1.5g, Cholesterol 5mg, Sodium 90mg, Total Carbohydrate 22g, Dietary Fiber 2g, Protein 7g*

peachy buttermilk *milkshake*

preparation: 15 minutes • **processing:** 20 seconds • **yield:** 4 1/2 cups (1.0 l) (4 servings)

2 cups (480 ml) low-fat buttermilk

1/8 teaspoon almond extract

2 cups (280 g) unsweetened frozen peach slices

2 cups (264 g) vanilla ice cream, softened

1. Place all ingredients into the Vitamix container in the order listed and secure lid.

2. Select Variable 1.

3. Switch machine to Start and slowly increase speed to Variable 10.

4. Blend for 20 seconds.

nutritional information: *Amount Per Serving: Calories 230, Total Fat 10g, Saturated Fat 6g, Cholesterol 35mg, Sodium 170mg, Total Carbohydrate 29g, Dietary Fiber 1g, Protein 8g*

green tea *smoothie*

---

preparation: 15 minutes • **processing:** 30 – 40 seconds • **yield:** 4 1/2 cups (1.0 l) (4 servings)

1 3/4 cups (420 ml) strong brewed green tea, cooled

1 Hass avocado, 8 ounces (227 g), halved, pitted, peeled

2 teaspoons honey

2 cups (60 g) fresh spinach leaves, lightly packed

3 cups (560 g) frozen green grapes

1 cup (240 ml) ice cubes

1. Place all ingredients into the Vitamix container in the order listed and secure lid.

2. Select Variable 1.

3. Switch machine to Start and slowly increase speed to Variable 10.

4. Blend for 30 to 40 seconds.

nutritional information: *Amount Per Serving: Calories 200, Total Fat 9g, Saturated Fat 1g, Cholesterol 0mg, Sodium 40mg, Total Carbohydrate 32g, Dietary Fiber 5g, Protein 1g*

strawberry *agua fresca*

preparation: 20 minutes • **processing:** 30–40 seconds • **yield:** 4 cups (960 ml) (4 servings)

4 cups (620 g) cubes, seeded watermelon

2 cups (300 g) fresh strawberries

2 Tablespoons (30 ml) fresh lemon juice

2 cups (480 ml) ice cubes

1. Place all ingredients into the Vitamix container in the order listed and secure lid.
2. Select Variable 1.
3. Switch machine to Start and slowly increase speed to Variable 10.
4. Blend for 30 seconds using the tamper to press the ingredients into the blades.

 nutritional information: *Amount Per Serving: Calories 60, Total Fat 0g, Saturated Fat 0g, Cholesterol 0mg, Sodium 10mg, Total Carbohydrate 20g, Dietary Fiber 2g, Protein 1g*

fruit salad *smoothie*

---

preparation: 20 minutes • ***processing:*** 30–40 seconds • ***yield:*** 4 1/4 cups (1.0 l) (4 servings)

1/2 cup (75 g) green grapes

1 medium orange, peeled, halved

1/2–inch-thick (1.3 cm) slice pineapple, core included, halved

1/2 cup (65 g) peeled and chopped cucumber

1 medium carrot, 2 1/2 ounces (71 g), halved

1 medium apple, 6 ounces (170 g), quartered, seeded

2 1/2 cups (600 ml) ice cubes

1. Place all ingredients into the Vitamix container in the order listed and secure lid.

2. Select Variable 1.

3. Switch machine to Start and slowly increase speed to Variable 10.

4. Blend for 30 to 40 seconds using the tamper to press the ingredients into the blades.

>> ***nutritional information:*** *Amount Per Serving: Calories 70, Total Fat 0g, Saturated Fat 0g, Cholesterol 0mg, Sodium 20mg, Total Carbohydrate 19g, Dietary Fiber 3g, Protein 1g*

blueberry pineapple *smoothie*

---

preparation: 15 minutes • ***processing:*** 30 – 40 seconds • ***yield:*** 2 1/2 cups (600 ml) (2 servings)

1/4 cup (60 ml) orange juice

1/4 cup (60 ml) pineapple juice

1/2 cup (120 g) low-fat vanilla yogurt

1 banana, peeled

2 cups (60 g) fresh spinach leaves, lightly packed

1 cup (140 g) frozen blueberries

1/4 cup (35 g) frozen dark sweet cherries

1/2 cup (120 ml) ice cubes

1. Place all ingredients into the Vitamix container in the order listed and secure lid.

2. Select Variable 1.

3. Switch machine to Start and slowly increase speed to Variable 10.

4. Blend for 30 to 40 seconds.

 nutritional information: *Amount Per Serving: Calories 190, Total Fat 1.5g, Saturated Fat 0.5g, Cholesterol 5mg, Sodium 85mg, Total Carbohydrate 43g, Dietary Fiber 5g, Protein 5g*

purple passion *smoothie*

preparation: 10 minutes • **processing:** 30–40 seconds • **yield:** 3 1/4 cups (780 ml) (3 servings)

1 1/2 cups (360 ml) pineapple juice

1 cup (240 g) low-fat vanilla yogurt

1 banana, peeled

1 cup (140 g) frozen unsweetened raspberries

1. Place all ingredients into the Vitamix container in the order listed and secure lid.
2. Select Variable 1.
3. Switch machine to Start and slowly increase speed to Variable 10.
4. Blend for 30 to 40 seconds.

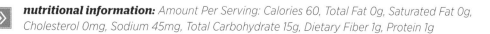 **nutritional information:** *Amount Per Serving: Calories 190, Total Fat 1g, Saturated Fat 0.5g, Cholesterol 5mg, Sodium 60mg, Total Carbohydrate 40g, Dietary Fiber 3g, Protein 5g*

minty green *smoothie*

preparation: 10 minutes • **processing:** 30–40 seconds • **yield:** 3 1/2 cups (840 ml) (3 servings)

1 cup (240 ml) water

4 cups (120 g) fresh spinach leaves

4 small mint leaves

2 1/2 cups (375 g) fresh pineapple chunks

1 1/2 cups (360 ml) ice cubes

1. Place all ingredients into the Vitamix container in the order listed and secure lid.
2. Select Variable 1.
3. Switch machine to Start and slowly increase speed to Variable 10.
4. Blend for 30 to 40 seconds.

nutritional information: *Amount Per Serving: Calories 60, Total Fat 0g, Saturated Fat 0g, Cholesterol 0mg, Sodium 45mg, Total Carbohydrate 15g, Dietary Fiber 1g, Protein 1g*

mocha spiced *hot cocoa*

---

preparation: 10 minutes • ***processing:*** 5 minutes • ***yield:*** 2 cups (480 ml) (2 servings)

1 1/2 cups (360 ml) milk

1/2 cup (90 g) semi-sweet chocolate chips

1/4 teaspoon ground cinnamon

2 teaspoons instant espresso

1/8 teaspoon chili powder

1. Place all ingredients into the Vitamix container in the order listed and secure lid.

2. Select Variable 1.

3. Switch machine to Start and slowly increase speed to Variable 10.

4. Blend for 5 minutes or until heavy steam escapes from the vented lid plug.

>> **nutritional information:** *Amount Per Serving: Calories 400, Total Fat 22g, Saturated Fat 13g, Cholesterol 20mg, Sodium 80mg, Total Carbohydrate 46g, Dietary Fiber 3g, Protein 10g*

apple *juice*

preparation: 10 minutes • **processing:** 45 seconds • **yield:** 1 cup (240 ml) strained (1 serving)

1 1/2 pounds (680 g) apples, cored, quartered

1/3 cup (80 ml) cool water

2 double layers of cheesecloth or nut milk filtration bag

1. Place apple and water into the Vitamix container in the order listed and secure lid.

2. Select Variable 1.

3. Switch machine to Start and slowly increase speed to Variable 10.

4. Blend for 45 seconds using the tamper to press the ingredients into the blades.

5. Dampen cheesecloth or filtration bag and squeeze out excess moisture. Transfer purée to a bowl lined with cheesecloth or filtration bag and twist until juice is extracted.

>> **nutritional information:** *Amount Per Serving: Calories 120, Total Fat 0g, Saturated Fat 0g, Cholesterol 0mg, Sodium 25mg, Total Carbohydrate 30g, Dietary Fiber 0g, Protein 0g*

cherry punch *cocktail*

preparation: 10 minutes • **processing:** 25 seconds • **yield:** 3 1/2 cups (840 ml) (3 servings)

2 ounces (60 ml) orange liqueur

1 ounce (30 ml) hazelnut liqueur

1 cup (140 g) frozen dark sweet cherries

1 cup (155 g) frozen tart cherries

2 cups (264 g) vanilla ice cream, softened

1. Place all ingredients into the Vitamix container in the order listed and secure lid.

2. Select Variable 1.

3. Switch machine to Start and slowly increase speed to Variable 8.

4. Blend for 25 seconds.

nutritional information: *Amount Per Serving: Calories 350, Total Fat 12g, Saturated Fat 7g, Cholesterol 35mg, Sodium 50mg, Total Carbohydrate 46g, Dietary Fiber 2g, Protein 5g*

spicy green mary *cocktail*

preparation: 15 minutes • **processing:** 30 seconds • **yield:** 4 servings

6 ounces (180 ml) vodka

8 ounces (227 g) English cucumber, cut into large chunks

2 Tablespoons (30 g) prepared horseradish

1 pound (454 g) tomatillos, husked, halved

1/8 teaspoon salt

1. Place all ingredients into the Vitamix container in the order listed and secure lid.

2. Select Variable 1.

3. Switch machine to Start and slowly increase speed to Variable 10.

4. Blend for 30 seconds.

5. Pour into ice-filled glasses and garnish with celery stalks.

>> **nutritional information:** *Amount Per Serving: Calories 150, Total Fat 1.5g, Saturated Fat 0g, Cholesterol 0mg, Sodium 100mg, Total Carbohydrate 10g, Dietary Fiber 3g, Protein 2g*

almond *milk*

---

preparation: 4 hours • ***processing:*** 45 seconds • ***yield:*** 3 1/2 cups (840 ml) (3 servings)

3 cups (720 ml) water

1 cup (140 g) raw almonds, soaked for at least 4 hours, drained

1. Place all ingredients into the Vitamix container in the order listed and secure lid.

2. Select Variable 1.

3. Switch machine to Start and slowly increase speed to Variable 10.

4. Blend for 45 seconds or until desired consistency is reached.

5. Store in refrigerator. Shake well before using.

 nutritional information: *Amount Per Serving: Calories 270, Total Fat 24g, Saturated Fat 2g, Cholesterol 0mg, Sodium 10mg, Total Carbohydrate 10g, Dietary Fiber 6g, Protein 10g*

rice *milk*

preparation: 45 minutes • **processing:** 2 1/2 – 3 minutes
yield: 2 1/2 cups (600 ml) (2 servings)

2 cups (480 ml) water

1/2 cup (100 g) cooked brown rice, cooled

1/2 Tablespoon brown sugar or other sweetener,
to taste

1. Place all ingredients into the Vitamix container in the order listed and secure lid.

2. Select Variable 1.

3. Switch machine to Start and slowly increase speed to Variable 10.

4. Blend for 2 1/2 to 3 minutes or until desired consistency is reached.

5. Store in refrigerator. Shake well before using.

 nutritional information: *Amount Per Serving: Calories 70, Total Fat 0g, Saturated Fat 0g, Cholesterol 0mg, Sodium 10mg, Total Carbohydrate 15g, Dietary Fiber 1g, Protein 1g*

straining non-dairy milks

Non-dairy milks are so easy to make in your Vitamix machine, and can be used over cereal, in baked goods, and to make creamy smoothies and ice creams. Many people enjoy non-dairy milks without straining, since they give added nutritional benefits. But to create a smoother, more commercial-style milk, you'll need to strain it. Simply place a fine mesh sieve or Vitamix nut milk filtration bag over a large bowl and pour the milk through it. If using a sieve, press milk with a spatula to strain it more rapidly. A filtration bag can be twisted to ensure you retrieve every last drop. The remaining fiber can be reserved for baking.

note: If you prefer a touch of sweetness, add 1/2 teaspoon vanilla extract with the other ingredients; pure vanilla extract provides the best flavor.

burst of berries *smoothie*

---

preparation: 10 minutes • **processing:** 45 seconds • **yield:** 2 1/2 cups (600 ml) (2 servings)

1/2 cup (120 ml) orange juice

1/2 cup (120 g) low-fat strawberry yogurt

1/2 cup (72 g) fresh strawberries

1 cup (140 g) frozen blackberries

1 cup (140 g) frozen blueberries

1/2 cup (120 ml) ice cubes

1. Place all ingredients into the Vitamix container in the order listed and secure lid.

2. Select Variable 1.

3. Switch machine to Start and slowly increase speed to Variable 10.

4. Blend for 45 seconds using the tamper to press the ingredients into the blades.

> **nutritional information:** *Amount Per Serving: Calories 180, Total Fat 1.5g, Saturated Fat 0g, Cholesterol 5mg, Sodium 40mg, Total Carbohydrate 41g, Dietary Fiber 6g, Protein 4g*

spring green *smoothie*

preparation: 15 minutes • **processing:** 45 seconds
yield: 4 3/4 cups (1.1 l) (4 servings)

1/4 cup (60 ml) water

1 1/2 cups (225 g) green grapes

1 orange, peeled, halved

1/2 lemon, peeled

1/2 cucumber, cut into large chunks

1/2 green apple, 3 1/2 ounces (99 g), halved, seeded

1 cup (67 g) kale, spine removed

1 cup (50 g) romaine lettuce

1 cup (60 g) parsley leaves

1 cup (150 g) frozen pineapple chunks

2 cups (480 ml) ice cubes

1. Place all ingredients into the Vitamix container in the order listed and secure lid.

2. Select Variable 1.

3. Switch machine to Start and slowly increase speed to Variable 10, using tamper if needed.

4. Blend for 45 seconds.

 **nutritional information:** *Amount Per Serving: Calories 90, Total Fat 0g, Saturated Fat 0g, Cholesterol 0mg, Sodium 20mg, Total Carbohydrate 21g, Dietary Fiber 4g, Protein 2g*

the riper the better

Most often when we're shopping for fruit, we look for slightly green produce so it doesn't spoil before we're able to use it. But for this recipe, the riper the apples and oranges, the sweeter the smoothie. Store green fruits at room temperature for a few days until they're fully ripened to enjoy the Spring Green Smoothie at its best.

frozen strawberry grape *smoothie*

preparation: 10 minutes • *processing:* 30 seconds • *yield:* 2 1/2 cups (600 ml) (2 servings)

1 cup (150 g) green grapes

1 cup (150 g) red grapes

1 cup (150 g) unsweetened frozen strawberries

1/2 cup (120 ml) ice cubes

1. Place all ingredients into the Vitamix container in the order listed and secure lid.

2. Select Variable 1.

3. Switch machine to Start and slowly increase speed to Variable 10.

4. Blend for 30 seconds using the tamper to press the ingredients into the blades.

>> *nutritional information:* Amount Per Serving: Calories 130, Total Fat 0g, Saturated Fat 0g, Cholesterol 0mg, Sodium 0mg, Total Carbohydrate 34g, Dietary Fiber 3g, Protein 2g

soy *milk*

ingredient IQ

For best flavor, source your soybeans from an Asian market or specialty store.

preparation: 8 hours • ***processing:*** 1 minute
cook time: 15 minutes • ***yield:*** 4 1/4 cups (1.0 l) (4 servings)

1 cup (200 g) dried soy beans

1 Tablespoon granulated sugar

3 1/2 cups (840 ml) water

1. Clean dried soy beans and soak in water for 4 to 8 hours. Steam for about 15 minutes.

2. Drain soy beans and let cool. Measure 1 1/2 cups (258 g) cooked beans.

3. Place cooked beans, sugar, and water into the Vitamix container in the order listed and secure lid.

4. Select Variable 1.

5. Switch machine to Start and slowly increase speed to Variable 10.

6. Blend for 1 minute or until desired consistency is reached.

7. To obtain commercial-style soy milk, strain the milk through a nut milk filtration bag or pass through a fine mesh sieve.

 ***nutritional information:*** *Amount Per Serving: Calories 120, Total Fat 6g, Saturated Fat 1g, Cholesterol 0mg, Sodium 10mg, Total Carbohydrate 10g, Dietary Fiber 4g, Protein 11g*

note: For a refreshing flavor, add a 1–inch (2.5 cm) cube of ginger root before blending.

sensational triple berry *smoothie*

preparation: 10 minutes • **processing:** 45 seconds • **yield:** 4 1/4 cups (1.0 l) (4 servings)

1 cup (240 ml) water

1 cup (245 g) low-fat vanilla yogurt

1 cup (150 g) red grapes

1 cup (150 g) frozen unsweetened strawberries

1 cup (150 g) frozen unsweetened blueberries

2 cups (240 g) frozen unsweetened raspberries

1. Place all ingredients into the Vitamix container in the order listed and secure lid.

2. Select Variable 1.

3. Switch machine to Start and slowly increase speed to Variable 10.

4. Blend for 45 seconds using the tamper to press the ingredients into the blades.

 **nutritional information:** *Amount Per Serving: Calories 120, Total Fat 1g, Saturated Fat 0.5g, Cholesterol 5mg, Sodium 45mg, Total Carbohydrate 26g, Dietary Fiber 3g, Protein 4g*

cherry berry
smoothie

preparation: 15 minutes • **processing:** 30–40 seconds
yield: 3 cups (720 ml) (3 servings)

1 cup (240 ml) pomegranate juice

6 ounces (170 g) fresh strawberries

1/2 cup (74 g) fresh blueberries

1 cup (123 g) fresh raspberries

1 cup (140 g) frozen dark sweet cherries

1. Place all ingredients into the Vitamix container in the order listed and secure lid.

2. Select Variable 1.

3. Switch machine to Start and slowly increase speed to Variable 10.

4. Blend for 30 to 40 seconds.

 **nutritional information:** *Amount Per Serving: Calories 130, Total Fat 0.5g, Saturated Fat 0g, Cholesterol 0mg, Sodium 10mg, Total Carbohydrate 31g, Dietary Fiber 5g, Protein 2g*

smoothies to spritzers

This smoothie is the perfect go-to recipe when you're hosting a shower or brunch. Prepare a glass of the original recipe for each of your guests. Then stir in sparkling water or champagne to create a bubbly berry spritzer. Either will create a festive beverage, while still affording your guests the option of alcoholic or virgin refreshment.

orange flax *smoothie*

preparation: 15 minutes • ***processing:*** 40 seconds • ***yield:*** 3 cups (720 ml) (3 servings)

1 cup (240 ml) carrot juice

1/2 cup (120 ml) orange juice

2 Tablespoons (13 g) ground flax seed

1 Tablespoon chopped fresh ginger root

2 cups (280 g) frozen unsweetened peach slices

1. Place all ingredients into the Vitamix container in the order listed and secure lid.
2. Select Variable 1.

3. Switch machine to Start and slowly increase speed to Variable 8.

4. Blend for 40 seconds.

>> **nutritional information:** *Amount Per Serving: Calories 100, Total Fat 1.5g, Saturated Fat 0g, Cholesterol 0mg, Sodium 20mg, Total Carbohydrate 21g, Dietary Fiber 3g, Protein 3g*

strawberry buttermilk *cooler*

preparation: 10 minutes • **processing:** 35 seconds • **yield:** 4 1/2 cups (1.0 l) (4 servings)

1 1/4 cups (300 ml) low-fat buttermilk

2 Tablespoons (30 ml) thawed orange juice concentrate

1/4 cup (30 g) powdered sugar

2 cups (300 g) fresh strawberries, hulled

4 cups (960 ml) ice cubes

1. Place all ingredients into the Vitamix container in the order listed and secure lid.

2. Select Variable 1.

3. Switch machine to Start and slowly increase speed to Variable 8.

4. Blend for 35 seconds.

>> **nutritional information:** *Amount Per Serving: Calories 100, Total Fat 1g, Saturated Fat 0g, Cholesterol 5mg, Sodium 90mg, Total Carbohydrate 20g, Dietary Fiber 1g, Protein 3g*

mocha *shake*

preparation: 20 minutes • ***processing:*** 20–25 seconds • ***yield:*** 4 cups (960 ml) (4 servings)

1/2 cup (120 ml) cold coffee

2 Tablespoons (30 ml) chocolate syrup

4 cups (528 g) vanilla ice cream

1 cup (240 ml) ice cubes

1. Place all ingredients into the Vitamix container in the order listed and secure lid.

2. Select Variable 1.

3. Switch machine to Start and slowly increase speed to Variable 8.

4. Blend for 20 to 25 seconds, using the tamper to press the ingredients into the blades.

>> ***nutritional information:*** *Amount Per Serving: Calories 330, Total Fat 18g, Saturated Fat 10g, Cholesterol 50mg, Sodium 80mg, Total Carbohydrate 36g, Dietary Fiber 0g, Protein 6g*

note: Allow ice cream to thaw at room temperature for 10 minutes before blending.

going green *smoothie*

preparation: 10 minutes • **processing:** 40 seconds
yield: 2 1/2 cups (600 ml) (2 servings)

1/2 cup (120 ml) water

1 cup (150 g) green grapes

1/2 cup (75 g) fresh pineapple chunks, core included

1/2 banana, peeled

2 cups (60 g) fresh spinach, lightly packed

1/2 cup (120 ml) ice cubes

1. Place all ingredients into the Vitamix container in the order listed and secure lid.

2. Select Variable 1.

3. Switch machine to Start and slowly increase speed to Variable 8.

4. Blend for 40 seconds.

 nutritional information: *Amount Per Serving: Calories 110, Total Fat 0g, Saturated Fat 0g, Cholesterol 0mg, Sodium 45mg, Total Carbohydrate 28g, Dietary Fiber 3g, Protein 2g*

start the day right

If you're new to green smoothies, this is a great beginner recipe. Even though it's packed with two cups of fresh spinach, all you taste is delicious, fresh fruit. Pair with the Savory Brunch Crêpes in the Breakfast section for a powerful start to your day.

whole fruit *margarita*

preparation: 15 minutes • ***processing:*** 40 seconds • ***yield:*** 6 cups (1.4 l) (6 servings)

1/4 cup (60 ml) water

6 ounces (180 ml) tequila

2 ounces (60 ml) Grand Marnier or triple sec

1 medium orange, peeled, halved

1 lime, peeled

1 lemon, peeled, halved

6 Tablespoons (75 g) granulated sugar

6 cups (1.4 l) ice cubes

1. Place all ingredients into the Vitamix container in the order listed and secure lid.

2. Select Variable 1.

3. Switch machine to Start and slowly increase speed to Variable 10.

4. Blend for 40 seconds or until desired consistency is reached.

5. Pour into salt-rimmed margarita glasses.

 nutritional information: *Amount Per Serving: Calories 150, Total Fat 0g, Saturated Fat 0g, Cholesterol 0mg, Sodium 10mg, Total Carbohydrate 20g, Dietary Fiber 1g, Protein 0g*

strawberry *daiquiri*

preparation: 10 minutes • **processing:** 30–40 seconds
yield: 3 cups (720 ml) (3 servings)

4 ounces (120 ml) light rum

2 ounces (60 ml) triple sec

2 Tablespoons (30 ml) fresh lime juice

1 cup (150 g) frozen strawberries, softened for 10 minutes

2–4 Tablespoons (16–32 g) powdered sugar

2 cups (480 ml) ice cubes

1. Place all ingredients into the Vitamix container in the order listed and secure lid.

2. Select Variable 1.

3. Switch machine to Start and slowly increase speed to Variable 8.

4. Blend for 30 to 40 seconds using the tamper to press the ingredients into the blades.

 nutritional information: *Amount Per Serving: Calories 180, Total Fat 0g, Saturated Fat 0g, Cholesterol 0mg, Sodium 0mg, Total Carbohydrate 19g, Dietary Fiber 1g, Protein 0g*

simple salting

Quickly and easily rim your margarita glasses with flavored sugars and cocktail salts using your Vitamix lid as a salt tray. Simply turn the lid upside down, and fill with about a 1/2–inch (1.3 cm) of sugar or salt. Wet the rims of glasses with a damp cloth, and twist slightly in the lid.

peachy keen *cocktail*

preparation: 15 minutes • **processing:** 30 seconds plus Pulsing
yield: 5 1/2 cups (1.3 l) (5 servings)

1/2 cup (120 ml) orange juice

1/2 cup (120 ml) light rum

6 ounces (170 g) thawed pink lemonade concentrate

3 fresh peaches, 10 1/2 ounces (300 g), halved, pitted

3 cups (720 ml) ice cubes

1. Place orange juice, rum, concentrate and peaches into the Vitamix container in the order listed and secure lid.

2. Select Variable 3.

3. Pulse 10 times.

4. Add ice to the Vitamix container and secure lid.

5. Select Variable 1.

6. Switch machine to Start and slowly increase speed to Variable 10.

7. Blend for 30 seconds.

 **nutritional information:** *Amount Per Serving: Calories 150, Total Fat 0g, Saturated Fat 0g, Cholesterol 0mg, Sodium 5mg, Total Carbohydrate 25g, Dietary Fiber 1g, Protein 1g*

islander *margarita*

preparation: 15 minutes • **processing:** 1 minute • **yield:** 1 serving

1/3 cup (80 ml) pineapple juice

1 ounce (30 ml) tequila

1/2 ounce triple sec

1 Tablespoon fresh lime juice

1 1/2 teaspoons grenadine

1/2 cup (93 g) frozen pineapple chunks, partially thawed

1/2 cup (93 g) frozen mango chunks, partially thawed

1 cup (240 ml) ice cubes

1. Place all ingredients into the Vitamix container in the order listed and secure lid.

2. Select Variable 1.

3. Switch machine to Start and slowly increase speed to Variable 10.

4. Blend for 1 minute, using the tamper to press the ingredients into the blades.

nutritional information: *Amount Per Serving: Calories 290, Total Fat 0g, Saturated Fat 0g, Cholesterol 0mg, Sodium 15mg, Total Carbohydrate 51g, Dietary Fiber 3g, Protein 1g*

chocolate covered
strawberry *milkshake*

preparation: 10 minutes • **processing:** 30 seconds • **yield:** 4 1/4 cups (1.0 l) (4 servings)

3 cups (400 g) nonfat vanilla Greek frozen yogurt

1/4 cup (60 ml) plus 2 Tablespoons (90 ml) skim milk

1 1/2 teaspoons vanilla extract

6 fresh strawberries, hulled

3 Tablespoons (45 g) chocolate milk powder

1. Place all ingredients into the Vitamix container in the order listed and secure lid.

2. Select Variable 1.

3. Switch machine to Start and slowly increase speed to Variable 8.

4. Blend for 30 seconds using the tamper to press the ingredients into the blades.

» **nutritional information:** *Amount Per Serving: Calories 190, Total Fat 0g, Saturated Fat 0g, Cholesterol 10mg, Sodium 120mg, Total Carbohydrate 34g, Dietary Fiber 1g, Protein 10g*

note: All the decadence of an old fashioned milkshake but without all of the fat and calories.

tropical *shake*

preparation: 15 minutes • **processing:** 40 seconds • **yield:** 3 1/4 cups (780 ml) (3 servings)

1 cup (240 ml) pineapple juice

3/4 cup (180 ml) soy milk

1/2 lemon, peeled

1 banana, frozen

1 cup (187 g) frozen mango chunks

1. Place all ingredients into the Vitamix container in the order listed and secure lid.

2. Select Variable 1.

3. Switch machine to Start and slowly increase speed to Variable 8.

4. Blend for 40 seconds.

» **nutritional information:** *Amount Per Serving: Calories 150, Total Fat 1g, Saturated Fat 0g, Cholesterol 0mg, Sodium 35mg, Total Carbohydrate 35g, Dietary Fiber 3g, Protein 3g*

blueberry *margarita*

preparation: 10 minutes • **processing:** 25–30 seconds • **yield:** 5 servings

1/2 cup (120 ml) simple syrup

1/2 cup (120 ml) orange juice

1/4 cup (60 ml) fresh lime juice

4 ounces (120 ml) tequila

1/2 cup (120 ml) blueberry juice

1 cup (148 g) fresh blueberries

4 cups (960 ml) ice cubes

1. Place all ingredients into the Vitamix container in the order listed and secure lid.
2. Select Variable 1.
3. Switch machine to Start and slowly increase speed to Variable 8.
4. Blend for 25 to 30 seconds.

 nutritional information: *Amount Per Serving: Calories 280, Total Fat 0g, Saturated Fat 0g, Cholesterol 0mg, Sodium 10mg, Total Carbohydrate 57g, Dietary Fiber 1g, Protein 0g*

old fashioned
vanilla *milkshake*

preparation: 10 minutes • **processing:** 15 seconds
yield: 4 3/4 cups (1.1 l) (4 servings)

4 cups (520 g) vanilla ice cream

1 3/4 cups (420 ml) milk

2 1/2 teaspoons vanilla extract

1. Place all ingredients into the Vitamix container in the order listed and secure lid.

2. Select Variable 1.

3. Switch machine to Start and slowly increase speed to Variable 8.

4. Blend for 15 seconds.

 nutritional information: *Amount Per Serving: Calories 340, Total Fat 18g, Saturated Fat 10g, Cholesterol 50mg, Sodium 115mg, Total Carbohydrate 36g, Dietary Fiber 0g, Protein 10g*

simple syrups

The easiest way to make simple syrup for the bar is to place equal parts of sugar and water into a sealed bottle and shake well. To create fruit-flavored syrups, place 3 cups of fresh fruit, 1/4 cup of sugar, and 1 teaspoon of lemon juice into the Vitamix container and blend on Variable 10 for 3 to 4 minutes. For a thicker, more traditional syrup, you can then place the mixture in a pot and simmer over medium heat for 30 minutes. Flavored syrups can be used in cocktails, over waffles and crêpes, or mixed with fruit juices and club soda for a refreshing virgin beverage.

cappuccino

preparation: 10 minutes • **processing:** 10 seconds • **yield:** 1 serving

3/4 cup (180 ml) hot double strength coffee

1/4 cup (60 ml) milk

2 Tablespoons (30 g) white chocolate chips

1/4 teaspoon vanilla extract

1. Place all ingredients into the Vitamix container in the order listed and secure lid.

2. Select Variable 1.

3. Switch machine to Start and slowly increase speed to Variable 8.

4. Blend for 10 seconds.

>> **nutritional information:** *Amount Per Serving: Calories 200, Total Fat 10g, Saturated Fat 8g, Cholesterol 5mg, Sodium 85mg, Total Carbohydrate 25g, Dietary Fiber 0g, Protein 2g*

vanilla coffee *frappé*

---

preparation: 15 minutes • **processing:** 10 seconds • **yield:** 2 1/2 cups (600 ml) (2 servings)

1 cup (240 ml) espresso, cooled

1/2 cup (120 ml) half & half

3 Tablespoons (38 g) granulated sugar

1 1/2 Tablespoons vanilla extract

1 1/4 cups (300 ml) ice cubes

1. Place all ingredients into the Vitamix container in the order listed and secure lid.
2. Select Variable 1.
3. Switch machine to Start and slowly increase speed to Variable 8.
4. Blend for 10 seconds or until desired consistency is reached.

>> **nutritional information:** *Amount Per Serving: Calories 190, Total Fat 7g, Saturated Fat 4.5g, Cholesterol 20mg, Sodium 50mg, Total Carbohydrate 25g, Dietary Fiber 0g, Protein 2g*

cider and whiskey *cocktail*

preparation: 10 minutes • **processing:** 15 seconds • **yield:** 1 serving

1/2 cup (120 ml) fresh apple cider

2 ounces (60 ml) bourbon whiskey

1 Tablespoon real maple syrup

1/4 small lemon, peeled

1 cup (240 ml) ice cubes

1. Place all ingredients into the Vitamix container in the order listed and secure lid.

2. Select Variable 1.

3. Switch machine to Start and slowly increase speed to Variable 5.

4. Blend for 15 seconds or until desired consistency is reached.

 nutritional information: *Amount Per Serving: Calories: 250, Total Fat: 0g, Saturated Fat: 0g, Cholesterol: 0g, Sodium 25mg, Total Carbohydrate 30g, Dietary Fiber 0g, Protein 0g*

piña colada *cocktail*

---

preparation: 10 minutes • **processing:** 40 seconds • **yield:** 3 1/2 cups (840 ml) (3 servings)

4 1/2 ounces (68 ml) light rum

4 1/2 Tablespoons (68 ml) cream of coconut

1/2 cup (120 ml) light coconut milk

2 Tablespoons (9 g) shredded coconut

3/4 cup (100 g) fresh pineapple chunks, core included

3 cups (720 ml) ice cubes

1. Place all ingredients into the Vitamix container in the order listed and secure lid.
2. Select Variable 1.
3. Switch machine to Start and slowly increase speed to Variable 5.
4. Blend for 40 seconds or until desired consistency is reached.

>> **nutritional information:** *Amount Per Serving: Calories 260, Total Fat 9g, Saturated Fat 8g, Cholesterol 0mg, Sodium 35mg, Total Carbohydrate 23g, Dietary Fiber 0g, Protein 1g*

pomarita *cocktail*

preparation: 10 minutes • **processing:** 30 seconds • **yield:** 3 cups (720 ml) (3 servings)

1/2 cup (120 ml) tequila

1 cup (240 ml) 100% pomegranate juice

1/4 cup (60 ml) triple sec

1/2 lime, peeled

2 Tablespoons (25 g) granulated sugar

2 cups (480 ml) ice cubes

1 fresh lime, thinly sliced

1. Place tequila, pomegranate juice, triple sec, lime, sugar and ice cubes into the Vitamix container in the order listed and secure lid.

2. Select Variable 1.

3. Switch machine to Start and slowly increase speed to Variable 10.

4. Blend for 30 seconds or until desired consistency is reached.

5. Serve in a chilled cocktail glass and garnish each serving with one or two thin slices of fresh lime.

> **nutritional information:** *Amount Per Serving: Calories 220, Total Fat 0g, Saturated Fat 0g, Cholesterol 0mg, Sodium 15mg, Total Carbohydrate 28g, Dietary Fiber 0g, Protein 0g*

frozen *bloody mary*

preparation: 10 minutes plus 5 hours freeze time • **processing:** Pulsing
yield: 4 1/2 cups (1.0 l) (4 servings)

3 cups (720 ml) tomato juice

1 cup (240 ml) beef broth

1 Tablespoon fresh lemon juice

1 teaspoon Worcestershire sauce

few drops hot sauce

1/2 cup (120 ml) vodka

1. Combine tomato juice, beef broth, lemon juice, Worcestershire sauce and hot sauce in a non-metal container. Cover and freeze for 5 hours.

2. Break up frozen mixture into large chunks.

3. Place into the Vitamix container, add vodka, and secure lid.

4. Select Variable 3.

5. Pulse a few times until slushy.

 **nutritional information:** *Amount Per Serving: Calories 120, Total Fat 0g, Saturated Fat 0g, Cholesterol 0mg, Sodium 740mg, Total Carbohydrate 9g, Dietary Fiber 1g, Protein 3g*

banana cream pie *milkshake*

preparation: 10 minutes • **processing:** 40 seconds • **yield:** 4 cups (960 ml) (4 servings)

1/4 cup (60 ml) plus 2 Tablespoons (30 ml) skim milk

3 cups (400 g) nonfat vanilla Greek frozen yogurt

1 banana, peeled, cut into large chunks

1/4 cup (21 g) plus 2 Tablespoons (11 g) graham cracker crumbs

1. Place all ingredients into the Vitamix container in the order listed and secure lid.

2. Select Variable 1.

3. Switch machine to Start and slowly increase speed to Variable 8.

4. Blend for 40 seconds using the tamper to press the ingredients into the blades.

 nutritional information: *Amount Per Serving: Calories 220, Total Fat 1g, Saturated Fat 0g, Cholesterol 10mg, Sodium 150mg, Total Carbohydrate 39g, Dietary Fiber 1g, Protein 11g*

strawberry white chocolate *milkshake*

preparation: 10 minutes • **processing:** 1 minute
yield: 4 1/2 cups (1.0 l) (4 servings)

1 cup (240 ml) skim milk

2 cups (268 g) nonfat vanilla Greek frozen yogurt

1/2 cup (120 g) white chocolate chips

2 cups (300 g) frozen unsweetened strawberries

1. Place all ingredients into the Vitamix container in the order listed and secure lid.

2. Select Variable 1.

3. Switch machine to Start and slowly increase speed to Variable 10.

4. Blend for 1 minute, using the tamper to press the ingredients into the blades.

 **nutritional information:** *Amount Per Serving: Calories 280, Total Fat 8g, Saturated Fat 7g, Cholesterol 5mg, Sodium 120mg, Total Carbohydrate 45g, Dietary Fiber 2g, Protein 9g*

healthy choices

Greek yogurt makes this milkshake a filling and satisfying snack or a decadent, guilt-free dessert. Since Greek yogurt has more protein, less sodium, and fewer carbohydrates than regular yogurt, it will help you feel fuller longer, while eliminating unnecessary fat and calories.

maple nut *milkshake*

preparation: 10 minutes • **processing:** 30 seconds • **yield:** 3 1/2 cups (840 ml) (3 servings)

3 cups (408 g) nonfat vanilla Greek frozen yogurt

1/4 cup (60 ml) plus 2 Tablespoons (30 ml) skim milk

1 1/2 teaspoons vanilla extract

3 Tablespoons (45 ml) maple syrup

1/4 cup (25 g) walnuts

1. Place all ingredients into the Vitamix container in the order listed and secure lid.
2. Select Variable 1.
3. Switch machine to Start and slowly increase speed to Variable 8.
4. Blend for 30 seconds using the tamper to press the ingredients into the blades.

>> **nutritional information:** *Amount Per Serving: Calories 330, Total Fat 6g, Saturated Fat 0.5g, Cholesterol 10mg, Sodium 150mg, Total Carbohydrate 51g, Dietary Fiber 1g, Protein 15g*

pineapple *milkshake*

preparation: 10 minutes • **processing:** 30 – 35 seconds
yield: 4 cups (960 ml) (4 servings)

1 cup (240 ml) pineapple juice

1 cup (240 ml) skim milk

2 1/2 cups (330 g) vanilla ice cream

2 cups (374 g) frozen pineapple chunks,
partially thawed

1/2 teaspoon ground cinnamon

1. Place all ingredients into the Vitamix container in the order listed and secure lid.

2. Select Variable 1.

3. Switch machine to Start and slowly increase speed to Variable 8, using the tamper if necessary.

4. Blend for 30 to 35 seconds.

 nutritional information: *Amount Per Serving: Calories 290, Total Fat 11g, Saturated Fat 6g, Cholesterol 30mg, Sodium 70mg, Total Carbohydrate 42g, Dietary Fiber 2g, Protein 6g*

milkshakes after five

A milkshake can easily become a fun frozen cocktail. Try a small amount of chocolate, vanilla, or coffee-flavored liqueur in your favorite milkshake recipes. For a more spirited addition, try rum to deepen the flavor of the Maple Nut and Pineapple Shakes, while bourbon livens up the Old Fashioned Vanilla and Banana Cream Pie Milkshakes. Be sure to stir in only a tablespoon or two of alcohol as too much will overpower the flavors and prevent the drink from freezing properly.

appetizers

appetizers

dips

fondues

hummus

salsas

appetizers

appetizers • dips • fondues • hummus • salsas

pineapple, pepper, and
pecan cheese *spread*

preparation: 15 minutes • **processing:** 30 seconds plus Pulsing
yield: 2 1/4 cups (540 ml) (18 servings)

11 ounces (312 g) cream cheese, softened

1/8 teaspoon cayenne pepper

3 green onions, cut in 1-inch (2.5 cm) pieces (white and pale green parts only)

1/2 green bell pepper, cut in 4 pieces

1/2 cup (83 g) fresh pineapple cubes

1/2 cup (50 g) pecan halves

1. Place cheese, cayenne pepper, and green onions into the Vitamix container and secure lid.

2. Select Variable 1.

3. Switch machine to Start and blend for 20 seconds. Stop machine and remove lid.

4. Add bell pepper to the Vitamix container and secure lid.

5. Select Variable 3.

6. Pulse 5 times. Stop machine and use rubber scraper to loosen food under blades.

7. Add pineapple to the Vitamix container and secure lid.

8. Select Variable 5.

9. Pulse 3 times, scraping sides of machine with rubber scraper once if necessary.

10. Add nuts to the Vitamix container and secure lid.

11. Select Variable 3.

12. Pulse 2 or 3 times.

13. Remove lid and scrape sides with a spatula. Loosen any pieces caught under the blades and secure lid.

14. Select Variable 1.

15. Switch machine to Start and blend 10 seconds.

16. Scrape into serving bowl or covered storage container. If desired, refrigerate several hours to blend flavors. May be stored in the refrigerator for 1 week. Serve with crackers or fresh vegetable crudités.

going beyond the bowl

Make your presentations just as appetizing as your dips by getting creative. A scooped-out pineapple half is a fun way to present fruit dips such as the Pineapple, Pepper and Pecan Cheese Spread.

nutritional information: *Amount Per 2 Tablespoon (30 g) Serving: Calories 80, Total Fat 7g, Saturated Fat 3g, Cholesterol 20mg, Sodium 75mg, Total Carbohydrate 2g, Dietary Fiber 0g, Protein 1g*

tuscan bean *dip*

preparation: 15 minutes • **processing:** 20 seconds plus Pulsing
yield: 3 cups (720 ml) (24 servings)

2 15–ounce (425 g) cans cannellini beans, rinsed, drained, divided use

2 Tablespoons (30 ml) fresh lemon juice

1/4 cup (60 ml) water

2 scallions, halved

2 garlic cloves, peeled

1/4 cup (28 g) oil packed sun-dried tomatoes, drained, finely chopped

1 Tablespoon fresh oregano or 1/2 teaspoon dried

1/2 teaspoon salt

1/2 teaspoon ground cumin

several dashes of hot sauce

1. Place one can drained beans, lemon juice, and water into the Vitamix container and secure lid.

2. Select Variable 1.

3. Switch machine to Start and slowly increase speed to Variable 6.

4. Blend for 20 seconds. Stop machine, scrape sides, and remove lid.

5. Place remaining can of beans, scallions, garlic, sun-dried tomatoes, oregano, salt, cumin and hot sauce into the Vitamix container and secure lid.

6. Select Variable 6.

7. Pulse 10 times.

 **nutritional information:** *Amount Per 2 Tablespoon (50 g) Serving: Calories 40, Total Fat 0g, Saturated Fat 0g, Cholesterol 0mg, Sodium 170mg, Total Carbohydrate 7g, Dietary Fiber 2g, Protein 3g*

note: Serve with artisan crackers or vegetables.

summer corn *cakes*

preparation: 20 minutes • **processing:** 25 seconds
cook time: 40 minutes • **yield:** 10 cakes

1/2 cup (62 g) whole wheat flour

1/2 teaspoon baking powder

1/2 cup (120 ml) milk

2 large eggs

2 Tablespoons (30 ml) canola oil, divided use

1/2 teaspoon salt

1/4 teaspoon freshly ground black pepper

1/2 cup (12 g) fresh basil leaves

2 cups (308 g) fresh corn kernels (from 2 large ears)

build a meal

A perfect way to utilize fresh corn in the summer, these Summer Corn Cakes make a delicious starter alongside a fresh salad or Tortilla Soup. Or top them with a tiny dollop of sour cream and a few thin slices of green onion to help them stand alone at your next barbeque.

tip: You can make your own fresh, whole wheat flour for this recipe in your Vitamix machine. Just grind 1 cup (200 g) of whole wheat berries for 1 minute on Variable 10.

1. Combine flour and baking powder in a medium-size mixing bowl. Set aside.

2. Place milk, eggs, 1 Tablespoon oil, salt, and pepper into the Vitamix container and secure lid.

3. Select Variable 1.

4. Switch machine to Start and blend for 10 seconds.

5. Remove lid plug and add basil through the lid plug opening. Blend an additional 10 seconds. Stop machine and remove lid.

6. Add corn kernels to the Vitamix container and secure lid.

7. Select Variable 1.

8. Switch machine to Start and blend 5 seconds. Pour wet mixture into dry ingredients and mix by hand to combine.

9. Heat remaining 1 Tablespoon oil in a large nonstick skillet over medium heat. Pour 1/4 cup (60 ml) batter for each cake. Cook until edges are dry, about 2 minutes. Flip and cook 2 minutes more, until golden brown.

nutritional information: *Amount Per Cake: Calories 90, Total Fat 4.5g, Saturated Fat 1g, Cholesterol 40mg, Sodium 160mg, Total Carbohydrate 11g, Dietary Fiber 1g, Protein 3g*

potstickers

preparation: 20 minutes • **processing:** Pulsing • **cook time:** 10 minutes per batch
yield: 60 potstickers (24 servings)

1 1/4 pounds (567 g) Chinese,
Napa, or Savoy cabbage, cut into
1 1/2–inch (4 cm) chunks, divided use

1 1/2 bunches green onions, washed,
halved, divided use

8 garlic cloves, peeled, divided use

1/2 cup (65 g) chopped fresh
ginger root, divided use

1/4 cup (60 ml) soy sauce

1 Tablespoon dark sesame oil

1 teaspoon fish sauce

1 package gyoza wrappers

1 teaspoon cornstarch mixed
with 1 Tablespoon cold water

1 Tablespoon canola oil

1. Place half of the cabbage, green onions, garlic, and ginger into the Vitamix container, float with water and secure lid.

2. Select Variable 10.

3. Pulse 5 times. Drain and repeat with the remaining half of ingredients. Place in large bowl.

4. Add soy sauce, sesame oil, and fish sauce to the chopped vegetables and mix by hand until evenly combined.

5. Lay gyoza wrappers flat and fill with about 1 to 1 1/2 teaspoons filling. Moisten a fingertip in the cornstarch and water mixture then rub along the edge of the dumpling. Pull bottom up and pinch together excess dumpling dough. Try to squeeze as much air out of the dumpling as you can while pinching sides. It will look like a pierogi. Press firmly together with a fork until it sticks.

6. Heat a heavy nonstick skillet with tight fitting lid over medium-high heat. Pour canola oil into skillet and swirl to coat the bottom. Sauté potstickers for 3 minutes. Add 1/2 cup (120 ml) warm water to the pan and immediately place the lid on the pan. If cooking them fresh, steam with the lid on for 5 minutes. If starting with frozen, steam for 8 minutes. When time is up, remove lid and cook an additional 1 to 2 minutes so the potstickers can brown.

7. Tightly wrap and freeze any remaining filling for next round of potsticker making.

plan ahead

Potstickers are great for quick appetizers, thanks to the Vitamix wet chop method. Make ahead and freeze in resealable bags; steaming just takes minutes. Serve with Carrot Ginger Vinaigrette Dressing as a dip. (For a refresher course on the wet chop method, refer to the Getting Started DVD that came with your Vitamix machine.)

nutritional information: *Amount Per Potsticker: Calories 25, Total Fat 0g, Saturated Fat 0g, Cholesterol 0mg, Sodium 120mg, Total Carbohydrate 4g, Dietary Fiber 0g, Sugars 0g, Protein 1g*

taco *guac*

---

preparation: 20 minutes • ***processing:*** 5–10 seconds • ***yield:*** 2 1/4 cups (540 ml) (18 servings)

8 ounces (227 g) tomatillos, husked, quartered

1/2 cup (8 g) fresh cilantro leaves

1 1/2 ounces (43 g) onion, peeled

1 1/2 ounces (43 g) jalapeño, halved, seeded

1 Tablespoon fresh lime juice

1 teaspoon kosher salt

2 garlic cloves, peeled

1 ripe Hass avocado, pitted, peeled

1. Place all ingredients into the Vitamix container in the order listed and secure lid.
2. Select Variable 1.
3. Switch machine to Start and slowly increase speed to Variable 5.
4. Blend for 5 to 10 seconds using the tamper to press the ingredients into the blades.

 nutritional information: *Amount Per 2 Tablespoon (26 g) Serving: Calories 20, Total Fat 1.5g, Saturated Fat 0g, Cholesterol 0mg, Sodium 110mg, Total Carbohydrate 2g, Dietary Fiber 1g, Protein 0g*

lentil *hummus*

preparation: 20 minutes • **processing:** 30–40 seconds
cook time: 15 minutes
yield: 4 cups (960 ml) (32 servings)

2 Tablespoons (22 g) kosher salt

1/2 pound (227 g) lentils, picked over

1/2 cup (120 g) tahini

5 garlic cloves, peeled

1/4 teaspoon salt

1/2 cup (120 ml) fresh lemon juice

3/4 cup (180 ml) water

1/2 cup (120 ml) extra virgin olive oil

1. In a large saucepan bring 2 quarts of water with salt and lentils to a boil and simmer about 15 minutes. Drain and rinse lentils under cold water, draining well.

2. Place lentils, tahini, garlic, salt, lemon juice, water and oil into the Vitamix container and secure lid.

3. Select Variable 1.

4. Switch machine to Start and slowly increase speed to Variable 10.

5. Blend for 30 to 40 seconds, using the tamper to press the ingredients into the blades.

6. Serve with toasted pita wedges, whole grain crackers, or fresh vegetables.

nutritional information: *Amount Per 2 Tablespoon (25 g) Serving: Calories 80, Total Fat 6g, Saturated Fat 1g, Cholesterol 0mg, Sodium 380mg, Total Carbohydrate 6g, Dietary Fiber 1g, Protein 2g*

dress up your dips

Hummus is a classic Middle Eastern dip that is a delicious source of protein on sandwiches, or served as an appetizer with pita, veggie, and whole-grain cracker dippers. For your next gathering, create a hummus platter, offering guests a variety of flavors to choose from, including Lentil, Hot Wing, Italian, and traditional Hummus (all shown in this section). Garnish each with its signature ingredient: a ring of lentils, a squirt of barbeque sauce, a tomato wedge with basil sprig, and a creative placement of chickpeas.

citrus fruit *dip*

preparation: 15 minutes • ***processing:*** 15 seconds • ***yield:*** 3 1/2 cups (840 ml) (28 servings)

3 cups (720 g) plain Greek yogurt

1/4 lime, peeled

1/8 orange, peeled

1/2-inch (1.3 cm) square piece lime peel or 1 Tablespoon lime zest

1/2-inch (1.3 cm) square piece orange peel or 1 Tablespoon orange zest

1/4 cup (60 ml) honey

1. Place all ingredients into the Vitamix container in the order listed and secure lid.
2. Select Variable 1.

3. Switch machine to Start and slowly increase speed to Variable 10.

4. Blend for 15 seconds.

5. Serve with fresh fruit as a dip or layer with granola and fruit for a delicious breakfast parfait.

>> **nutritional information:** *Amount Per 2 Tablespoon (29 g) Serving: Calories 40, Total Fat 2.5g, Saturated Fat 2g, Cholesterol5mg, Sodium 5mg, Total Carbohydrate 3g, Dietary Fiber 0g, Protein 2g*

note: Peel citrus fruit with a vegetable peeler to avoid getting the bitter white pith.

smoky chile *salsa*

preparation: 20 minutes • **processing:** Pulsing • **yield:** 1 1/2 cups (360 ml) (12 servings)

1/4 cup (60 ml) red wine vinegar

1/4 cup (60 ml) extra virgin olive oil

2 teaspoons chipotles in adobo sauce

7 ounce (200 g) ripe tomato, quartered

2 ounce (56 g) onion wedge, peeled

1 jalapeño, halved, seeded

1/4 cup (4 g) fresh cilantro leaves

1. Place all ingredients into the Vitamix container in the order listed and secure lid.

2. Select Variable 6.

3. Pulse 5 times. Stop machine and scrape sides of container. Replace lid and pulse 3 more times.

4. Season to taste with salt and pepper before serving. Serve with tortilla chips or fresh vegetables.

>> **nutritional information:** *Amount Per 2 Tablespoon (33 g) Serving: Calories 45, Total Fat 4.5g, Saturated Fat 0.5g, Cholesterol 0mg, Sodium 5mg, Total Carbohydrate 1g, Dietary Fiber 0g, Protein 0g*

note: This salsa pairs nicely with carnitas or steak tacos.

italian *hummus*

preparation: 15 minutes • **processing:** 45 seconds • **yield:** 3 cups (720 ml) (24 servings)

3 cups (720 g) canned chickpeas, drained, rinsed; 1/2 cup (120 ml) liquid reserved

2–3 garlic cloves, peeled

1/4 cup (60 g) tahini

1/4 cup (60 ml) fresh lemon juice

1/4 cup (60 g) tomato paste

1 Tablespoon extra virgin olive oil

2 teaspoons dried oregano

1 teaspoon dried basil

1/2 teaspoon kosher salt

1. Place all ingredients into the Vitamix container in the order listed and secure lid.

2. Select Variable.

3. Switch machine to Start and slowly increase speed to Variable 10.

4. Blend for 45 seconds, using the tamper to press the ingredients into the blades. Serve with breadsticks or serve atop crostini. Garnish with olive slice.

 nutritional information: *Amount Per 2 Tablespoon (28 g) Serving: Calories 50, Total Fat 2.5g, Saturated Fat 0g, Cholesterol 0mg, Sodium 90mg, Total Carbohydrate 6g, Dietary Fiber 0g, Protein 2g*

salsa verde

---

preparation: 20 minutes • **processing:** 20 seconds plus Pulsing
yield: 2 1/2 cups (600 ml) (20 servings)

1–2 slices fresh bread

1/4 cup (60 ml) red wine vinegar

2 cups (120 g) packed parsley leaves

1 cup (240 ml) olive oil

2 Tablespoons (18 g) capers, drained

2 Tablespoons (16 g) pine nuts

20 pitted green olives

4 anchovy filets

2 garlic cloves, peeled

2 hard-boiled egg yolks

1. Tear bread into pieces, place into the Vitamix container and secure lid.

2. Select Variable 6.

3. Pulse 5 times. Measure out 2/3 cup (30 g) and place into the Vitamix container. Place the rest in a sealed container; store in a cool, dry place.

4. Place remaining ingredients into the Vitamix container and secure lid.

5. Select Variable 1.

6. Switch machine to Start and slowly increase speed to Variable 7.

7. Blend for 10 seconds. Stop and scrape down sides. Blend an additional 10 seconds to obtain desired consistency.

 nutritional information: *Amount Per 2 Tablespoon (33 g) Serving: Calories 130, Total Fat 13g, Saturated Fat 2g, Cholesterol 20mg, Sodium 180mg, Total Carbohydrate 2g, Dietary Fiber 0g, Protein 1g*

guacamole *dip*

preparation: 15 minutes • ***processing:*** Pulsing • ***yield:*** 2 1/2 cups (600 ml) (20 servings)

1 Roma tomato, 3 ounces (85 g), quartered, divided use

4 ripe Hass avocados, halved, pitted, peeled, divided use

1/2 cup (40 g) chopped red onion

2 Tablespoons (30 ml) fresh lemon juice

1/2 cup (8 g) fresh cilantro leaves

1 teaspoon salt

1. Place 1/2 tomato, 2 avocados, onion, lemon juice, cilantro and salt into the Vitamix container in the order listed and secure lid.

2. Select Variable 6.

3. Pulse until ingredients are mixed, using the tamper to push the ingredients into the blades while processing.

4. Remove lid, add remaining avocado and tomato and secure lid.

5. Select Variable 5.

6. Pulse 8 to 10 times until ingredients are mixed, using the tamper to push the ingredients into the blades while processing.

7. Do not over blend. Leave chunky. Serve with tortilla chips.

» **nutritional information:** *Amount Per 2 Tablespoon (38 g) Serving: Calories 50, Total Fat 4g, Saturated Fat 0.5g, Cholesterol 0mg, Sodium 120mg, Total Carbohydrate 3g, Dietary Fiber 2g, Protein 1g*

peppercorn *cheese cubes*

preparation: 20 minutes • **processing:** 20–30 seconds • **yield:** 3/4 cup (180 ml) (12 servings)

3/4 cup (180 ml) extra virgin olive oil

2-inch (5 cm) strip lemon peel

1 lemon, halved, peeled

3 garlic cloves, peeled

1 1/2 teaspoons dried whole peppercorns

1 teaspoon fennel seeds

1 pound (454 g) Monterey Jack or provolone cheese, cut into 3/4-inch (1.9 cm) chunks

1. Place oil, lemon peel, lemon, garlic, peppercorns and fennel seeds into the Vitamix container and secure lid.

2. Select Variable 1.

3. Switch machine to Start and slowly increase speed to Variable 10.

4. Blend for 20 to 30 seconds.

5. Place cheese cubes into a sealable plastic bag. Pour the marinade over the cheese and refrigerate for up to 3 days. Let stand 1 hour at room temperature prior to serving.

» **nutritional information:** *Amount Per Serving: Calories 270, Total Fat 25g, Saturated Fat 9g, Cholesterol 35mg, Sodium 200mg, Total Carbohydrate 1g, Dietary Fiber 0g, Protein 9g*

note: Peel citrus fruit with a vegetable peeler to avoid getting the bitter white pith.

hot wing *hummus*

preparation: 15 minutes • **processing:** 45 seconds • **yield:** 3 cups (720 ml) (24 servings)

3 cups (720 g) canned chickpeas, drained, rinsed; 1/2 cup (120 ml) liquid reserved

2–3 garlic cloves, peeled

1/4 cup (60 g) tahini

1/4 cup (60 ml) fresh lemon juice

1 Tablespoon white vinegar

1–2 Tablespoons barbecue sauce

3 Tablespoons (45 ml) hot sauce

1 1/2 teaspoons paprika

1/4 teaspoon kosher salt

1. Place all ingredients into the Vitamix container in the order listed and secure lid.
2. Select Variable 1.
3. Switch machine to Start and slowly increase speed to Variable 10.
4. Blend for 45 seconds, using the tamper to press the ingredients into the blades. Serve with celery and carrot sticks.

 nutritional information: *Amount Per 2 Tablespoon (28 g) Serving: Calories 45, Total Fat 2g, Saturated Fat 0g, Cholesterol 0mg, Sodium 115mg, Total Carbohydrate 6g, Dietary Fiber 0g, Protein 2g*

note: The type of hot sauce used will impact the spice of this dip. Dial heat up or down with your favorite hot sauce selection, or offer a range of options for guests with two to three heat levels to choose from.

southwest black bean *dip*

preparation: 15 minutes • **processing:** 30–40 seconds
yield: 2 cups (480 ml) (16 servings)

1/4 cup (60 ml) water

1 Tablespoon fresh lemon juice

2 Tablespoons (2 g) fresh cilantro leaves

2 garlic cloves, peeled

15–ounce (425 g) can black beans, drained, rinsed

1 Tablespoon balsamic vinegar

1 teaspoon ground cumin

1/2 teaspoon chili powder

dash salt

dash ground black pepper

1. Place all ingredients into the Vitamix container in the order listed and secure lid.

2. Select Variable 1.

3. Switch machine to Start and slowly increase speed to Variable 7.

4. Blend for 30 to 40 seconds, using the tamper to press the ingredients into the blades.

5. Garnish with chopped cilantro and serve with tortilla chips or fresh vegetables.

 nutritional information: *Amount Per 2 Tablespoon (36 g) Serving: Calories 30, Total Fat 0g, Saturated Fat 0g, Cholesterol 0mg, Sodium 115mg, Total Carbohydrate 5g, Dietary Fiber 2g, Protein 2g*

make it fiesta night

A great source of protein, Southwest Black Bean Dip can be used in a variety of dishes. For a self-serve, weeknight meal, create a build-your-own taco bar. Offer both soft and crispy tortilla shells, and let everyone choose their favorite fillings, such as grilled chicken, ground beef and onion mixture, and Southwest Black Bean Dip. You could also include Taco Guac and California Salsa (also shown in this section), followed by shredded lettuce, cheeses, and sour cream. The best part is, all these ingredients will refrigerate well in sealed containers, so you can serve an encore performance later in the week.

sweet papaya *salsa*

---

preparation: 20 minutes • ***processing:*** Pulsing • ***yield:*** 2 cups (480 ml) (16 servings)

4 ounce (114 g) tomato, quartered

1/2 jalapeño, seeded

2 Tablespoons (2 g) cilantro leaves

1 ounce (28 g) shallot

14 ounces (400 g) ripe papaya, seeded, peeled

1 garlic clove, peeled

2 Tablespoons (30 ml) fresh lime juice

1 teaspoon grated lime zest

1/2 cup (82 g) frozen corn

3 Tablespoons (20 g) flax seed meal

2 teaspoons whole flax seed

1. Place all ingredients into the Vitamix container in the order listed and secure lid.

2. Select Variable 5.

3. Pulse 10 times using the tamper to press the ingredients into the blades. If necessary, stop and scrape sides with a spatula. Pulse 5 more times.

 nutritional information: *Amount Per 2 Tablespoon (32 g) Serving: Calories 25, Total Fat 0.5g, Saturated Fat 0g, Cholesterol 0mg, Sodium 0mg, Total Carbohydrate 5g, Dietary Fiber 1g, Protein 1g*

selecting ripe papaya

First, look for fruits that are predominantly yellow. Watch for soft or sunken spots; papaya should have a pliable, but not overly soft skin. A ripe papaya fruit should have a light, sweet smell. Eat ripe papaya immediately, or refrigerate in a plastic bag to halt the ripening process. Don't freeze papaya, as it harms the texture and flavor of the fruit.

spinach artichoke *dip*

preparation: 20 minutes • **processing:** 25 seconds • **bake time:** 20–25 minutes
yield: 2 3/4 cups (660 ml) (22 servings)

1/2 cup (120 g) light mayonnaise

1/2 cup (120 g) reduced fat sour cream

1/4-inch (.6 cm) slice lemon, peeled

10-ounce (284 g) package frozen spinach, thawed, drained

1/8 teaspoon salt

1/8 teaspoon ground black pepper

1 garlic clove, peeled

1/4 cup (50 g) grated Parmesan cheese

1/2 cup (85 g) canned artichoke hearts, drained

1. Preheat oven to 350°F (180°C).

2. Place mayonnaise, sour cream, lemon, spinach, salt, black pepper, garlic, and Parmesan cheese into the Vitamix container and secure lid.

3. Select Variable 1.

4. Switch machine to Start and slowly increase speed to Variable 6.

5. Blend for 15 seconds. Remove the lid plug and add artichokes through the lid plug opening. Replace lid plug and blend an additional 10 seconds.

6. Pour into an oven-safe dish and bake uncovered 20 to 25 minutes or until bubbly.

>> **nutritional information:** *Amount Per 2 Tablespoon (29 g) Serving: Calories 35, Total Fat 2.5g, Saturated Fat 1g, Cholesterol 5mg, Sodium 115mg, Total Carbohydrate 2g, Dietary Fiber 0g, Protein 1g*

traditional cheese *fondue*

preparation: 15 minutes • **processing:** 4 minutes
yield: 4 cups (960 ml) (32 servings)

3/4 cup (180 ml) dry white wine

3/4 cup (180 ml) water

1 1/2 Tablespoons Kirsch

2 Tablespoons (16 g) cornstarch

1/4 teaspoon nutmeg

1 teaspoon ground black pepper

8 ounces (227 g) Gruyere cheese,
cut into 1–inch (2.5 cm) cubes

8 ounces (227 g) Emmental cheese,
cut into 1–inch (2.5 cm) cubes

1. Place all ingredients into the Vitamix container in the order listed and secure lid.

2. Select Variable 1.

3. Switch machine to Start and slowly increase speed to Variable 10.

4. Blend for 4 minutes or until mixture is smooth and warm. Pour mixture into fondue pot.

nutritional information: Amount Per 2 Tablespoon (26 g) Serving: Calories 70, Total Fat 4.5g, Saturated Fat 2.5g, Cholesterol 15mg, Sodium 50mg, Total Carbohydrate 1g, Dietary Fiber 0g, Protein 4g

planning ahead

Turn weekend leftovers into weeknight dinner. Fondues are such a simple way to make a big impact when entertaining. This Traditional Cheese Fondue is a delicious precursor to any dinner spread. Offer your guests cubed country French bread, apple slices, or steamed asparagus spears, broccoli, or cauliflower. Leftover fondue can be used to make an excellent base for a soup or pasta sauce.

cost-cutting tip:
Substitue Swiss for Emmental cheese for a more cost-effective, yet still smooth and delicious fondue.

california *salsa*

preparation: 15 minutes • **processing:** Pulsing • **yield:** 2 1/4 cups (540 ml) (18 servings)

1/2 medium onion, 2 1/2 ounces (70 g), peeled, halved

1 jalapeño pepper, 1 1/2 ounces (43 g), seeded

1/4 cup (4 g) fresh cilantro leaves

1 teaspoon fresh lemon juice

1/2 teaspoon salt

6 ripe Roma tomatoes, quartered (24 quarters)

1. Place onion, jalapeño, cilantro, lime, salt and six of the tomato quarters into the Vitamix container in the order listed and secure lid.

2. Select Variable 5.

3. Pulse 2 times.

4. Add the remaining tomato quarters through the lid plug opening. Continue to Pulse until desired consistency is reached, about 5 times.

5. Serve with tortilla chips.

>> **nutritional information:** *Amount Per 2 Tablespoon (28 g) Serving: Calories 5, Total Fat 0g, Saturated Fat 0g, Cholesterol 0mg, Sodium 65mg, Total Carbohydrate 1g, Dietary Fiber 0g, Protein 0g*

chili-cheese *fondue*

preparation: 20 minutes • **processing:** 4 minutes • **yield:** 3 1/2 cups (840 ml) (28 servings)

8 ounces (227 g) cubed cheddar cheese

8 ounces (227 g) cubed Monterey Jack cheese

2 garlic cloves, peeled

3/4 cup (180 ml) milk

4-ounce (113 g) can chopped green chilies

2 Tablespoons (30 ml) tequila

1. Place all ingredients into the Vitamix container in the order listed and secure lid.

2. Select Variable 1.

3. Switch machine to Start and slowly increase speed to Variable 10, using the tamper to press the ingredients into the blades.

4. Blend for 4 minutes.

>> **nutritional information:** *Amount Per 2 Tablespoon (30 g) Serving: Calories 70, Total Fat 5g, Saturated Fat 3.5g, Cholesterol 15mg, Sodium 160mg, Total Carbohydrate 1g, Dietary Fiber 0g, Protein 5g*

note: Serve with tortilla chips, cubed rustic breads, cauliflower florets, broccoli florets, or asparagus spears.

hummus *dip*

---

preparation: 15 minutes • ***processing:*** 30–40 seconds
yield: 2 1/2 cups (600 ml) (20 servings)

1/4 cup (60 ml) fresh lemon juice

1/4 cup (60 ml) water

2 15-ounce (425 g) cans chickpeas (garbanzos), one drained, one with liquid

1/4 cup (35 g) raw sesame seeds

1 Tablespoon olive oil

1 garlic clove, peeled

1 teaspoon ground cumin

1/2 teaspoon salt

1. Place all ingredients into the Vitamix container in the order listed and secure lid.

2. Select Variable 1.

3. Switch machine to Start and slowly increase speed to Variable 10.

4. Blend for 30 to 40 seconds, using tamper if needed.

nutritional information: *Amount Per 2 Tablespoon (29 g) Serving: Calories 30, Total Fat 1g, Saturated Fat 0g, Cholesterol 0mg, Sodium 105mg, Total Carbohydrate 4g, Dietary Fiber 1g, Protein 1g*

surprise visitors

Hummus is the new "basic black dress" of the kitchen. Dress it up on a cracker with olive slices and parsley, or use as a healthy sub for mayo in a sandwich.

soups

soups

bisque • chili • chowder • soups

crab *bisque*

preparation: 25 minutes • ***processing:*** 30–40 seconds • ***cook time:*** 30–35 minutes
yield: 4 3/4 cups (1.1 l) soup and 2 cups (480 g) relish (4 servings)

relish:

1 medium tomato, 5 ounces
(142 g), quartered

1 cup (154 g) fresh corn kernels or
frozen, thawed

1 small avocado, pitted, peeled

1 Tablespoon lime juice

1/4 teaspoon salt

dash freshly ground black pepper

bisque:

1 Tablespoon extra virgin olive oil

1 cup (154 g) fresh corn kernels or frozen, thawed

1 cup (160 g) rough chop onion

1 cup (150 g) rough chop yellow bell pepper

1 1/2 cups (225 g) unpeeled, rough chop Russet potato

3/4 teaspoon sweet or hot smoked paprika

1 cup (240 ml) dry sherry

2 cups (480 ml) clam juice

2 cups (480 ml) 2% milk

12 ounces (340 g) crab meat, rinsed

1/2 teaspoon salt

1. Place tomato, corn, avocado, lime juice, salt, and pepper into the Vitamix container and secure lid.

2. Select Variable 1.

3. Pulse 3 to 4 times. Stop, scrape down sides and repeat process until desired consistency is reached. Set aside.

4. Heat oil in a large saucepan over medium heat. Add corn, onion, bell pepper and cook, stirring often, until the onion and pepper have softened, about 5 minutes.

5. Add potato and paprika and cook, stirring often, for 2 minutes. Add sherry and cook, scraping up any browned bits until the liquid has reduced slightly, about 5 minutes. Add clam juice and bring to a boil. Reduce heat and simmer, until the potatoes are tender, about 15 minutes. Remove from heat and let cool 15 minutes.

6. Place mixture into the Vitamix container and secure lid.

7. Select Variable 1.

8. Switch machine to Start and slowly increase speed to Variable 8.

9. Blend for 30 to 40 seconds.

10. Return purée to the saucepan. Stir in milk, crab meat, and salt. Cook, stirring occasionally, until heated through, 3 to 5 minutes.

11. Serve topped with relish and sprinkled with paprika.

>> **nutritional information:** *Amount Per Serving: Calories 460, Total Fat 13g, Saturated Fat 3g, Cholesterol 80mg, Sodium 1400mg, Total Carbohydrates 45g, Dietary Fiber 6g, Protein 25g*

note: To easily remove fresh corn from the cob, cut enough off one tip to create a flat top. Stand cob upright and using a sharp knife, cut downwards through two or three rows of kernels. Repeat until all kernels are removed.

basic sweet potato *soup*

preparation: 25 minutes • **processing:** 5 minutes 45 seconds • **cook time:** 10 minutes
yield: 6 cups (1.4 l) (6 servings)

4 cups (960 ml) chicken broth

1 pound (454 g) sweet potatoes

3 Tablespoons (45 ml) orange juice

1/2 teaspoon orange zest

1/4 teaspoon ground nutmeg

1/4 cup (60 ml) half & half

1. Pierce sweet potatoes several times with a knife and place in microwave. Cook on High for 7 to 10 minutes or until fork tender. Remove from microwave and let cool. Peel and quarter potatoes.

2. Place chicken broth, sweet potatoes, orange juice, orange zest, and nutmeg into the Vitamix container and secure lid.

3. Select Variable 1.

4. Switch machine to Start and slowly increase speed to Variable 10.

5. Blend for 5 minutes 45 seconds. Reduce speed to Variable 2 and remove the lid plug.

6. Add half & half through the lid plug opening. Replace lid plug and blend an additional 10 seconds.

>> **nutritional information:** *Amount Per Serving: Calories 100, Total Fat 1.5g, Saturated Fat 1g, Cholesterol 5mg, Sodium 680mg, Total Carbohydrates 18g, Dietary Fiber 3g, Protein 3g*

acorn squash *soup*

preparation: 15 minutes
processing: 5 minutes 45 seconds
yield: 4 cups (960 ml) (4 servings)

2 cups (480 ml) chicken broth

1/2 cup (120 ml) low-fat evaporated milk

1/2 medium acorn squash, cooked, peeled, seeded, cooled

1 teaspoon maple syrup

pinch ground nutmeg

1/4 teaspoon ground cinnamon

salt and ground black pepper

kitchen prep

To save time, here's a quick way to cook acorn squash for this recipe. Cut squash in half, remove seeds, and place face down in a microwaveable dish. Add water to cover the bottom of the dish. Cover and microwave on High until tender, about 7 minutes. Let cool and scoop out flesh.

1. Place chicken broth, milk, squash, maple syrup, nutmeg, and cinnamon into the Vitamix container in the order listed and secure lid.

2. Select Variable 1.

3. Switch machine to Start and slowly increase speed to Variable 10.

4. Blend for 5 minutes 45 seconds.

5. Reduce speed to Variable 1 and remove the lid plug. Pour evaporated milk through the lid plug opening.

6. Blend for an additional 10 seconds. Season to taste with salt and pepper.

nutritional information: Amount Per Serving: Calories 70, Total Fat 1g, Saturated Fat 0g, Cholesterol 10mg, Sodium 530mg, Total Carbohydrates 12g, Dietary Fiber 2g, Protein 3g

sweet potato broccoli *soup*

preparation: 20 minutes • ***processing:*** 1 minute • ***cook time:*** 30 minutes
yield: 7 3/4 cups (1.8 l) (7 servings)

2 Tablespoons (30 ml) extra virgin olive oil

1 medium onion, 3 1/2 ounces (99g),
rough chop

2 stalks celery, 6 ounces (170 g), rough chop

2 cups (480 ml) reduced sodium
chicken broth

1 cup (240 ml) half & half

1/2 pound (227 g) Russet potatoes, quartered

1 pound (454 g) sweet potatoes,
peeled, quartered

1 bay leaf

1 cup (240 ml) water

kosher salt and ground black pepper

3 cups (213 g) broccoli florets

3 Tablespoons (45 ml) water

1/3 pound (151 g) shredded sharp cheddar

1. Heat the olive oil in a large pot over medium-high heat. Add the onion and celery and cook, stirring until softened, about 5 minutes. Add the broth, half & half, Russet and sweet potatoes, bay leaf, water, 1 teaspoon salt, and 1/4 teaspoon ground black pepper; bring to a boil.

2. Reduce heat to medium low and simmer until the potatoes are tender, about 10 minutes. Meanwhile, put the broccoli in a microwave safe bowl, add 3 Tablespoons (45 ml) water, cover and microwave on High 4 minutes, or until crisp tender.

3. When potatoes are tender, remove from heat, and let cool 40 minutes. Remove bay leaf.

4. Place mixture into the Vitamix container and secure lid.

5. Select Variable 1.

6. Switch machine to Start and slowly increase speed to Variable 7.

7. Blend for 1 minute.

8. Pour back into pot and heat over medium heat until hot. Add broccoli and cheddar cheese. Stir until cheese is melted.

>> ***nutritional information:*** *Amount Per Serving: Calories 230, Total Fat 12g, Saturated Fat 5g, Cholesterol 25mg, Sodium 360mg, Total Carbohydrates 23g, Dietary Fiber 4g, Protein 9g*

vegetable *soup* and *pesto*

preparation: 30 minutes • **processing:** 1 minute 10 seconds • **cook time:** 30 minutes
yield: 12 1/2 cups (3.0 l) (12 servings)

soup:

1/3 cup (80 ml) extra virgin olive oil

5 garlic cloves, peeled, halved

3 medium carrots, 9 ounces (256 g), coarse chop

2 stalks celery, 5 ounces (142 g), coarse chop

1 medium yellow onion, 3 1/2 ounces (100 g), coarse chop

1/2 medium zucchini, 4 1/2 ounces (128 g), coarse chop

1/4 head Savoy cabbage, 7 1/2 ounces (200 g), coarse chop

8 cups (1.9 l) chicken broth

7 whole, peeled canned tomatoes or 14-ounce (397 g) can diced tomatoes

15 ounce (425 g) can cannellini beans, drained, divided use

1/2 pound (227 g) thin spaghetti, cooked

1. Heat oil in a large sauce pan over medium high heat. Add garlic, carrots, celery, and onions. Cook covered, stirring occasionally until crisp tender, 12 to 15 minutes.

2. Add zucchini and cabbage. Cook covered until wilted, 3 to 5 minutes.

3. Add broth and tomatoes. Bring to a boil and cook for 5 minutes. Take off heat and cool for 20 minutes.

4. Place half of the soup and half of the beans into the Vitamix container and secure lid.

5. Select Variable 1.

6. Switch machine to Start and slowly increase speed to Variable 8.

7. Blend for 30 to 40 seconds. Return mixture to pot, add remaining beans, and bring back up to a simmer.

8. Serve over cooked spaghetti with a Tablespoon of pesto.

pesto:

1/4 cup (60 ml) extra virgin olive oil

1 medium plum tomato, 5 1/2 ounces (156 g)

4 cups (96 g) packed basil leaves

1 cup (100 g) grated Parmesan

1 teaspoon kosher salt

2 garlic cloves, peeled

1. Place all ingredients into the Vitamix container in the order listed and secure lid.

2. Select Variable 1.

3. Switch machine to Start and slowly increase speed to Variable 6.

4. Blend for 30 seconds, using the tamper to press the ingredients into the blades.

nutritional information: *Amount Per Serving: Calories 320, Total Fat 16g, Saturated Fat 3.5g, Cholesterol 10mg, Sodium 690mg, Total Carbohydrates 32g, Dietary Fiber 5g, Protein 13g*

beet *soup*

preparation: 15 minutes • ***processing:*** 5 minutes 45 seconds • ***cook time:*** 30 minutes
yield: 5 cups (1.2 l) (5 servings)

1 Tablespoon olive oil

2 garlic cloves, peeled, chopped

4 ounces (114 g) Russet potato, quartered

1 3/4 pounds (794 g) canned beets, drained (2 15-ounce (425 g) cans)

3 1/2 cups (840 ml) chicken broth

1 Tablespoon fresh dill

1/2 teaspoon kosher salt

1/8 teaspoon ground black pepper

sour cream and fresh dill for garnish

1. In a saucepan, sauté garlic in olive oil over medium heat for 1 minute. Add potato and cook for 5 minutes. Add beets and chicken broth; bring to a boil. Reduce heat, cover, and simmer for 20 minutes. Remove from heat and cool 20 minutes.

2. Place beets mixture, fresh dill, salt, and pepper into the Vitamix container and secure lid.

3. Select Variable 1.

4. Switch machine to Start and slowly increase speed to Variable 10.

5. Blend for 5 minutes 45 seconds. Ladle into bowls and garnish with sour cream and dill sprig.

>> **nutritional information:** *Amount Per Serving: Calories 100, Total Fat 3g, Saturated Fat 0g, Cholesterol 0mg, Sodium 910mg, Total Carbohydrates 17g, Dietary Fiber 3g, Protein 4g*

clam *chowder*

preparation: 20 minutes • ***processing:*** 30 seconds • ***cook time:*** 40 minutes
yield: 6 1/2 cups (1.5 l) (6 servings)

2 pounds (908 g) chopped clam
meat, rinsed

2 cups (480 ml) clam juice

10 ounces (284 g) Russet potatoes cut
into 1/2-inch (1.3 cm) cubes

1 slice bacon, chopped

1 medium onion, 5 ounces (142 g),
rough chop

1 stalk celery, 3 ounces (85 g), rough chop

2 bay leaves

2 garlic cloves, peeled, rough chop

1 teaspoon fresh thyme

1 cup (240 ml) half & half

4 teaspoons unsalted butter, sliced

2 Tablespoons (8 g) chopped fresh parsley

2 Tablespoons (6 g) chopped fresh chives

1/2 teaspoon paprika

1. Bring 2 cups (480 ml) clam juice and clams to a simmer. Remove clams with
   a slotted spoon and set aside.

2. Add potatoes to the clam juice and simmer until tender, about 10 to 15 minutes. Remove
   from heat. Cool 15 minutes.

3. While potatoes are cooking, sauté bacon over medium heat until crisp. Add onion, celery,
   and bay leaves; cook until soft, about 3 minutes. Add garlic and thyme; cook 3 minutes.
   Cool slightly and remove bay leaves.

4. Place 1/3 of the potatoes, simmering liquid and cooked vegetables to the Vitamix container
   and secure lid.

5. Select Variable 1.

6. Switch machine to Start and slowly increase speed to Variable 7.

7. Blend for 30 seconds.

8. Pour back into pot, add clam meat, reserved potato, and stir in half & half. Heat on medium-low heat for 15 minutes.

9. Pour into bowls and garnish with a teaspoon of butter, parsley, chives, and paprika.

 nutritional information: *Amount Per Serving: Calories 260, Total Fat 9g, Saturated Fat 4.5g, Cholesterol 70mg, Sodium 1140mg, Total Carbohydrates 19g, Dietary Fiber 1g, Protein 26g*

note: Look for low-sodium clam juice to avoid unwanted salt.

planning ahead

Since you can make at least four servings of soup in your Vitamix machine with a single blend, freezing your favorite soups is an easy way to be prepared for weeknight meals or lunches in a pinch. It's also a great way to use up every last bit of produce from the market before it spoils. Store soups in family-size or individual portions, making it easy for kids to help themselves after school.

cream of asparagus *soup*

preparation: 25 minutes • **processing:** 5 minutes 30 seconds • **yield:** 4 cups (960 ml) (4 servings)

1 1/2 pounds (680 g) asparagus spears (reserve 1 cup (180 g) pieces for garnish)

1 1/2 cups (360 ml) chicken broth

1/8 teaspoon salt

1/8 teaspoon ground black pepper

1/2 cup (120 ml) heavy cream

1. Steam asparagus in a small amount of water until tender, about 10 minutes. Drain. Cool to room temperature. Set aside 1 cup (180 g) asparagus pieces for garnish.

2. Place asparagus, chicken broth, salt, and pepper into the Vitamix container and secure lid.

3. Select Variable 1.

4. Switch machine to Start and slowly increase speed to Variable 10.

5. Blend for 5 minutes or until smooth.

6. Reduce speed to Variable 1 and remove the lid plug. Pour in heavy cream through the lid plug opening.

7. Slowly increase speed to Variable 10 and blend for an additional 30 seconds. Serve immediately over reserved asparagus pieces.

herbology

Fresh herbs such as parsley, basil, or chervil impart extra flavor, allowing you to adjust the taste of creamy soups without adding extra salt.

nutritional information: *Amount Per Serving: Calories 140, Total Fat 12g, Saturated Fat 7g, Cholesterol 41mg, Sodium 640mg, Total Carbohydrates 4g, Dietary Fiber 3g, Protein 7g*

leek, artichoke and potato *soup*

preparation: 20 minutes • **processing:** 30-40 seconds • **cook time:** 35-40 minutes
chill time: 2 hours • **yield:** 7 1/2 cups (1.8 l) (7 servings)

2 Tablespoons (30 ml) olive oil

2 cups (180 g) leeks, white parts chopped (2 medium)

9 garlic cloves, peeled

2 cups (480 ml) vegetable broth

2 9.9-ounce (281 g) jars artichoke hearts in water, rinsed, drained

6 ounces (170 g) Russet potatoes, cut into 1-inch (2.5 cm) chunks

6 fresh thyme sprigs, leaves removed

2 cups (480 ml) water

2 teaspoons lemon juice

6 Tablespoons (90 g) Kale and Basil Pesto (see sauces & spreads)

1. Heat oil in a large saucepan over medium heat. Add leeks and garlic; sauté for 5 minutes or until leeks are softened and translucent. Add broth, artichokes, potatoes, thyme leaves, and 2 cups (480 ml) water. Cover and bring to a boil.

2. Reduce heat to medium low; simmer partially covered for 20 to 25 minutes or until potatoes are tender. Cool for 40 minutes.

3. Place mixture into the Vitamix container, add lemon juice, and secure lid.

4. Select Variable 1.

5. Switch machine to Start and slowly increase speed to Variable 8.

6. Blend for 30 to 40 seconds.

7. Pour into a soup pot and bring up to temperature over medium heat. Divide into bowls and garnish with 1 Tablespoon of Kale Basil Pesto.

nutritional information: *Amount Per Serving: Calories 180, Total Fat 11g, Saturated Fat 1.5g, Cholesterol 5mg, Sodium 590mg, Total Carbohydrates 16g, Dietary Fiber 1g, Protein 5g*

white onion apple *soup*

preparation: 25 minutes • **processing:** 30–40 seconds • **cook time:** 30 minutes
yield: 7 cups (1.7 l) (7 servings)

2 Tablespoons (30 ml) olive oil

1 1/2 cups (240 g) chopped white onion

1 1/4 pounds (568 g) carrots, quartered

3 3/4 cups (900 ml) reduced sodium
chicken broth

1 Fuji apple, cored, quartered, divided use

2 teaspoons chopped fresh ginger root

4 1/2 Tablespoons (68 ml) frozen apple juice
concentrate, thawed

1/4 teaspoon grated nutmeg

1/4 teaspoon ground allspice

kosher salt

ground black pepper

chopped fresh mint

1. Heat olive oil in a large saucepan over medium-high heat. Add onion; sauté 2 minutes. Add carrots, broth, 2 apple quarters and ginger. Bring to a boil. Cover and reduce heat. Simmer until carrots are tender, 20 minutes. Remove from heat and let cool 40 minutes.

2. Place soup into the Vitamix container and secure lid.

3. Select Variable 1.

4. Switch machine to Start and slowly increase speed to Variable 8.

5. Blend for 30 to 40 seconds.

6. Return soup to saucepan and add apple juice, nutmeg, and allspice; heat until hot. Season to taste with salt and pepper. Chop remaining apple. Ladle soup into bowls and garnish with diced apple and mint.

nutritional information: *Amount Per Serving: Calories 120, Total Fat 4g, Saturated Fat 0.5g, Cholesterol 0mg, Sodium 350mg, Total Carbohydrates 20g, Dietary Fiber 4g, Protein 3g*

winter squash *soup* with spiced *pepitas*

preparation: 30 minutes • **processing:** 35–40 seconds • **cook time:** 20–25 minutes
yield: 6 1/4 cups (1.5 l) (6 servings)

spiced pepitas:

1/2 cup (69 g) pepitas

1 Tablespoon olive oil

2 teaspoons agave nectar

1/2 teaspoon smoked paprika

1/2 teaspoon salt

2 Tablespoons (2 g) chopped fresh cilantro

1. Preheat oven to 350°F (180°C). Line baking sheet with silpat or parchment paper. Toss pepitas with olive oil, agave, paprika, and salt in a small bowl. Spread on baking sheet and bake for 10 to 12 minutes, turning occasionally. Cool. Break into pieces and toss with chopped cilantro. Set aside.

soup:

1 Tablespoon olive oil

4 1/2 ounces (128 g) onion, rough chop (1 medium)

2 garlic cloves, peeled, halved

2 teaspoons smoked paprika

1 bay leaf

2 Tablespoons (30 ml) dry sherry

1 1/2 pounds (680 g) winter squash, peeled, seeded, cut into 1–inch (2.5 cm) pieces

2 cups (480 ml) vegetable broth

1 cup (240 ml) water

picking winter squash

Any winter squash will work well in this recipe, such as acorn, butternut, kabocha, or delicata. Always select winter squash that seem heavy for their size. Look for clean, thick skin with no scuffs or blemishes. For the squash to keep well, you want a piece of the vine to still be attached, and the skin should not give when pressed.

1. Heat oil in a large pot over medium-high heat. Add onion, sauté for 3 to 5 minutes, then stir in garlic, smoked paprika, and bay leaf. Cook for 1 minute.

2. Add sherry, cook 2 minutes. Add squash, broth, and water. Bring to a simmer, cover, and reduce heat to medium-low. Cook 20 minutes, or until squash is tender. Remove from heat and let cool 30 minutes. Remove bay leaf.

3. Place mixture into the Vitamix container and secure lid.

4. Select Variable 1.

5. Switch machine to Start and slowly increase speed to Variable 10.

6. Blend for 35 to 40 seconds.

7. Pour into pot and heat over medium heat for 5 minutes.

nutritional information: *Amount Per Serving: Calories 160, Total Fat 10g, Saturated Fat 1.5g, Cholesterol 0mg, Sodium 540mg, Total Carbohydrates 17g, Dietary Fiber 3g, Protein 4g*

chestnut *soup*

preparation: 20 minutes • **processing:** 35–40 seconds • **cook time:** 35 minutes
yield: 8 cups (1.9 l) (8 servings)

soup:

2 Tablespoons (28 g) unsalted butter

1 medium onion, 4 ounces (114 g), rough chop

1 stalk celery, 3 ounces (85 g), rough chop

1 medium carrot, 3 1/2 ounces (99 g), rough chop

1 garlic clove, peeled

1/2 teaspoon kosher salt

4 cups (960 ml) reduced sodium chicken broth

2 cups (480ml) water

1 bay leaf

15–ounce (425 g) jar roasted chestnuts, drained

1/2 cup (120 ml) heavy cream

1 Tablespoon dry sherry

croutons:

3 Tablespoons (42 g) unsalted butter

2 cups (256 g) cubed rustic bread, crusts removed

1/2 teaspoon saffron threads

1. Melt the 2 Tablespoons (28 g) butter in a large saucepan over medium heat. Add the onion, celery, carrot, garlic, and salt. Cook until soft, about 8 minutes.

2. Add chicken broth, water, and bay leaf. Bring to a boil, then reduce heat to medium-low and simmer 5 minutes.

3. Add chestnuts and simmer until chestnuts and vegetables are tender, about 10 minutes. Remove from heat and let cool 40 minutes. Remove bay leaf.

4. Place half of the mixture into the Vitamix container and secure lid.

5. Select Variable 1.

6. Switch machine to Start and slowly increase speed to Variable 8 for 35 to 40 seconds.

7. Pour into a large saucepan and repeat with remaining half. Bring up to temperature over medium heat.

8. Meanwhile, melt 3 Tablespoons (42 g) butter in a skillet over medium heat. Add the bread and cook, stirring until golden, about 3 minutes. Add the saffron and cook until the croutons are browned.

9. Ladle into bowls and garnish with croutons.

ingredient IQ

Simmering the chestnuts and vegetables browns their edges and brings out a roasted, more robust flavor, giving this soup a hearty feel.

nutritional information: *Amount Per Serving: Calories 170, Total Fat 13g, Saturated Fat 8g, Cholesterol 40mg, Sodium 360mg, Total Carbohydrates 10g, Dietary Fiber 1g, Protein 3g*

chicken potato spinach *soup*

preparation: 15 minutes • **processing:** 5 minutes 45 seconds
yield: 5 1/4 cups (1.2 l) (5 servings)

1 cup (240 ml) chicken broth

1 1/2 cups (360 ml) milk

1/4 cup (40 g) chopped onion

3 medium Russet potatoes (640 g), baked, halved, divided use

1/8 teaspoon dried rosemary

1 Tablespoon spinach, cooked or frozen, thawed

5 ounces (140 g) skinless, boneless chicken breast, cooked and diced

salt to taste

1. Place broth, milk, onion, two potatoes, and rosemary into the Vitamix container in the order listed and secure lid.

2. Select Variable 1.

3. Switch machine to Start and slowly increase speed to Variable 8.

4. Blend for 5 minutes 30 seconds.

5. Reduce speed to Variable 1 and remove the lid plug.

6. Add spinach, remaining potato, and chicken through the lid plug opening. Replace lid plug and blend an additional 10 to 15 seconds.

create your own

This recipe is a great use for leftover chicken. Be sure to use Russet potatoes as they are less waxy. Other potatoes become gummy when blended.

Easily convert this soup to a vegetarian recipe by omitting the chicken and using vegetable broth.

nutritional information: *Amount Per Serving: Calories 213, Total Fat 6g, Saturated Fat 1g, Cholesterol 16mg, Sodium 353mg, Total Carbohydrates 30g, Dietary Fiber 3g, Protein 10g*

leafy green *soup*

preparation: 20 minutes • **processing:** 40–60 seconds • **cook time:** 1 hour
yield: 9 1/2 cups (2.2 l) (9 servings)

2 Tablespoons (30 ml) extra virgin olive oil

9 ounces (255 g) yellow onion, rough chop

1 teaspoon salt, divided use

2 Tablespoons (30 ml) plus 3 cups (720 ml) water, divided use

1/4 cup (48 g) uncooked Arborio rice

1 pound (454 g) green chard, white ribs removed, rough chop (1 bunch)

14 cups (420 g) gently packed spinach leaves, rough chop

4 cups (960 ml) vegetable broth

large pinch of cayenne pepper

1 Tablespoon lemon juice

1. Heat oil in a large skillet over high heat. Add onions and 1/4 teaspoon salt; cook, stirring frequently until the onions begin to brown, about 5 minutes. Reduce heat to low, add 2 Tablespoons (30 ml) water and cover. Cook, stirring frequently until the pan cools down, then occasionally, always covering the pan, until the onions reduce and have a deep caramel color, 25 to 30 minutes.

2. Combine 3 cups (720 ml) water and 3/4 teaspoon salt in a Dutch oven. Add rice and bring to a boil. Reduce heat; cover and simmer for 15 minutes. Stir in chard, return to a simmer, cover and cook for 10 minutes. Add cooked onions, spinach, broth, and cayenne. Return to a simmer, cover cook, stirring once until spinach is tender, 5 minutes. Remove from heat and let cool 50 minutes.

3. Place half the mixture into the Vitamix container and secure lid.

4. Select Variable 1.

5. Switch machine to Start and slowly increase speed to Variable 10.

6. Blend for 20 to 30 seconds. Pour into a soup pot and repeat with remaining half of mixture. Heat over medium heat until hot. Stir in 1 Tablespoon lemon juice prior to serving.

>> **nutritional information:** *Amount Per Serving: Calories 90, Total Fat 3g, Saturated Fat 0g, Cholesterol 0mg, Sodium 840mg, Total Carbohydrates 14g, Dietary Fiber 3g, Protein 2g*

thyme for tomato *soup*

preparation: 15 minutes
processing: 6 minutes
yield: 4 cups (960 ml) (4 servings)

1/2 ounce (15 g) onion, peeled

1 garlic clove, peeled

3/4 cup (83 g) oil-packed sun-dried tomatoes, drained

14 1/2-ounce (410 g) can diced tomatoes

1 1/4 cups (300 ml) water

1 Tablespoon fresh thyme sprigs

1 Tablespoon double concentrated tomato paste

1/2 extra large vegetable bouillon cube

1/4 cup (60 ml) heavy cream

1. Place onion, garlic, sun-dried tomatoes, tomatoes, water, thyme, tomato paste, and bouillon cube into the Vitamix container and secure lid.

2. Select Variable 1.

3. Switch machine to Start and slowly increase speed to Variable 10.

4. Blend for 5 minutes 45 seconds. Reduce speed to Variable 1 and remove lid plug.

5. Add heavy cream through the lid plug opening and replace lid plug.

6. Slowly increase speed to Variable 10.

7. Blend for 20 seconds.

 nutritional information: *Amount Per Serving: Calories 130, Total Fat 9g Saturated Fat 4g, Cholesterol 20mg, Sodium 420mg, Total Carbohydrates 12g, Dietary Fiber 2g, Protein 2g*

ingredient IQ

Sun-dried tomatoes are a great source of rich, unique flavor brought out through a slow aging process. Add them to the top of the finished soup for a mouth-watering garnish.

creamy tomato *soup*

preparation: 15 minutes • **processing:** 6 minutes 5 seconds • **cook time:** 20 – 25 minutes
yield: 6 3/4 cups (1.6 l) (6 servings)

2 Tablespoons (28 g) unsalted butter

1/4 cup (40 g) chopped onion

1/2 teaspoon salt

1/8 teaspoon ground black pepper

2 14 1/2-ounce (410 g) cans diced tomatoes

1 Tablespoon granulated sugar

1 teaspoon Worcestershire sauce

2 cups (480 ml) half & half

Fresh basil for garnish

1. Melt butter in a medium saucepan until it starts to brown; add onion. Cook over medium heat until onion is softened, 5 minutes, stirring frequently.
    Stir in salt and pepper.

2. Place onion mixture, tomatoes, sugar, and Worcestershire sauce into the Vitamix container and secure lid.

3. Select Variable 1.

4. Switch machine to Start and slowly increase speed to Variable 10.

5. Blend for 5 minutes 45 seconds.

6. Reduce speed to Variable 1 and remove the lid plug. Add half & half through the lid plug opening. Replace lid plug.

7. Slowly increase speed to Variable 10. Blend for 30 seconds.

8. Garnish with freshly ground black pepper and fresh chopped basil and serve.

>> **nutritional information:** *Amount Per Serving: Calories 180, Total Fat 13g, Saturated Fat 8g, Cholesterol 40mg, Sodium 580mg, Total Carbohydrates 13g, Dietary Fiber 1g, Protein 4g*

note: Garnish with fresh chopped basil.

winter greens *soup*

preparation: 20 minutes • **processing:** 30 seconds plus Pulsing • **cook time:** 25 – 30 minutes
yield: 11 1/2 cups (2.8 l) (11 servings)

2 leeks, trimmed, halved, sliced

4 1/2 ounces (128 g) celery, rough chop (2 stalks)

2 garlic cloves, peeled

1 Tablespoon olive oil

5 1/4 cups (1.2 l) vegetable broth

14 1/2–ounce (410 g) can diced tomatoes

4 cups (268 g) chopped kale

17 1/2 ounces (497 g) zucchini, halved, sliced

1/4 teaspoon salt

1/4 teaspoon ground black pepper

5 ounces (142 g) fresh baby spinach

1/2 cup (30 g) Italian parsley or basil

2 Tablespoons (30 ml) red wine vinegar

Chopped tomato and basil for garnish

1. In a large Dutch oven, sauté leeks, celery, and garlic in oil over medium heat for 10 minutes. Stir in broth, tomatoes, kale, zucchini, salt, and pepper. Bring to a boil. Reduce heat and simmer covered, 5 minutes, stirring once. Remove from heat and let cool 50 minutes.

2. Place 2/3 of the mixture into the Vitamix container and secure lid.

3. Select Variable 1.

4. Switch machine to Start and slowly increase speed to Variable 10.

5. Blend for 30 seconds. Pour into pot.

6. Repeat with remaining soup. After blending, remove lid and add in fresh spinach, parsley and vinegar and secure lid.

7. Select Variable 6.

8. Pulse 5 times. Pour into pot containing other blended soup. Heat over medium-high heat for 5 minutes before serving.

nutritional information: *Amount Per Serving: Calories 70, Total Fat 1.5g, Saturated Fat 0g, Cholesterol 0mg, Sodium 630mg, Total Carbohydrates 11g, Dietary Fiber 2g, Protein 3g*

note: Garnish with chopped tomatoes and basil.

bright idea

You can buy pre-chopped kale in large bags in the produce section. Use leftover kale in your favorite green smoothie, combining a small amount with spinach or other leafy greens at first, and increasing the kale gradually to allow your tastebuds to adjust to the bolder flavor.

velvety fennel *soup*

preparation: 20 minutes • ***processing:*** 30 seconds plus Pulsing • ***cook time:*** 30 – 35 minutes
yield: 3 1/2 cups (840 ml) (3 servings)

2 Tablespoons (30 ml) extra virgin olive oil, divided use

2 cups (174 g) chopped fennel bulb, chop and reserve fronds

1 cup (124 g) diced zucchini

1 cup (160 g) chopped onion

1/4 teaspoon fennel seeds

2 cups (480 ml) reduced sodium chicken broth

3/4 cup (112 g) grape tomatoes

1. Heat 1 1/2 Tablespoons olive oil in a large saucepan over medium heat. Add fennel bulb, zucchini, onion, and fennel seeds. Sauté until fennel is translucent, 5 to 6 minutes.

2. Add broth and bring to a boil. Cover, reduce heat and simmer until vegetables are tender, about 15 minutes. Remove from heat and let cool 15 minutes.

3. For tomato garnish, place tomatoes into the Vitamix container and secure lid.

4. Select Variable 5.

5. Pulse 2 to 3 times to chop tomatoes. Transfer to a heated 9–inch (23 cm) skillet. Add remaining olive oil and sauté tomatoes until heated through, 1 to 2 minutes. Remove from heat and add 1 Tablespoon chopped fennel fronds. Season to taste with salt and ground black pepper. Remove from container and set aside.

6. Place fennel, zucchini and onion mixture into the Vitamix container and secure lid.

7. Select Variable 1.

8. Switch machine to Start and slowly increase speed to Variable 8.

9. Blend for 30 seconds.

10. Return to saucepan and heat over medium heat until hot. Serve soup garnished with warm tomato garnish.

>> ***nutritional information:*** *Amount Per Serving: Calories 150, Total Fat 10g, Saturated Fat 1.5g, Cholesterol 0mg, Sodium 410mg, Total Carbohydrates 13g, Dietary Fiber 4g, Protein 5g*

curried cauliflower *soup*

preparation: 20 minutes • **processing:** 45 seconds • **cook time:** 30 minutes
yield: 7 1/2 cups (1.8 l) (7 servings)

2 Tablespoons (30 ml) olive oil

1 medium onion, 5 ounces (142 g),
rough chop

1 medium tart apple, 7 ounces (200 g),
cored, quartered

1 Tablespoon curry powder

1 garlic clove, peeled

6 cups (600 g) cauliflower, chopped into
1–inch (2.5 cm) pieces (1 large head)

4 cups (960 ml) vegetable broth

1 teaspoon agave nectar

1 teaspoon rice wine vinegar

1. Heat oil in a large pot over medium-high heat. Add onion and sauté 5 to 7 minutes or until soft and golden. Stir in apple, curry powder, and garlic. Cook an additional 2 minutes until curry turns deep yellow.

2. Add cauliflower and broth then bring to a simmer. Cover, reduce heat to medium-low and simmer 20 minutes. Cool 20 minutes.

3. Place mixture into the Vitamix container and secure lid.

4. Select Variable 1.

5. Switch machine to Start and slowly increase speed to Variable 8.

6. Blend for 35 to 40 seconds.

7. Reduce speed to Variable 1 and remove the lid plug.

8. Pour agave nectar and vinegar through the lid plug opening. Replace lid plug and blend an additional 10 seconds.

» **nutritional information:** *Amount Per Serving: Calories 90, Total Fat 4.5g, Saturated Fat 0.5g, Cholesterol 0mg, Sodium 570mg, Total Carbohydrates 14g, Dietary Fiber 3g, Protein 2g*

note: Garnish with diced apples.

sweet potato sage *soup*

preparation: 35 minutes • **processing:** 1 minute 15 seconds • **cook time:** 1 hour
yield: 11 1/2 cups (2.8 l) (11 servings)

3 Tablespoons (45 ml) extra virgin olive oil, divided use

1 cup (160 g) diced onion

1 teaspoon salt, divided use

2 Tablespoons (30 ml) plus 4 cups (960 ml) water, divided use

4 garlic cloves, peeled, halved

1 teaspoon chopped fresh thyme leaves

1 large bunch kale, tough stems removed, coarse chop

1 pound (454 g) sweet potatoes, peeled, cut into 1-inch (2.5 cm) cubes

8 fresh sage leaves

12 ounces (340 g) fresh spinach

4 cups (960 ml) vegetable broth

pinch cayenne pepper

pinch ground black pepper

1 Tablespoon fresh lemon juice

1 Tablespoon agave nectar

1. Heat 2 Tablespoons (30 ml) oil in a skillet over high heat. Add onion and 1/4 teaspoon salt. Cook, stirring frequently, until the onions begin to brown, about 5 minutes. Reduce heat to low, stir in 2 Tablespoons (30 ml) water, garlic, and thyme. Cover and cook, stirring frequently until the pan cools down, then occasionally, always covering the pan, until the onions reduce and have a deep caramel color, 25 to 30 minutes.

2. Meanwhile, combine 4 cups (960 ml) water and 3/4 teaspoon salt in a Dutch oven; add kale, sweet potato, and sage. Bring to a boil. Reduce heat to maintain a simmer; cover and cook 15 minutes.

3. Stir in spinach, return to a simmer, cover and cook for 10 minutes more. When the onions are caramelized, stir a little simmering liquid into them, scrape up any browned bits, and add to the soup. Add vegetable broth, return to a simmer. Cook for 5 minutes more. Remove from heat and let cool 40 minutes.

4. Place half the mixture into the Vitamix container and secure lid.

5. Select Variable 1.

6. Switch machine to Start and slowly increase speed to Variable 8.

7. Blend for 35 to 40 seconds. Pour into soup pot and repeat with remaining half. Stir in cayenne, ground black pepper, lemon juice, and agave nectar.

 nutritional information: *Amount Per Serving: Calories 100, Total Fat 4g, Saturated Fat 0.5g, Cholesterol 0mg, Sodium 610mg, Total Carbohydrates 16g, Dietary Fiber 3g, Protein 3g*

gazpacho *soup*

preparation: 20 minutes • **processing:** 10 seconds plus Pulsing • **chill time:** 1-2 hours
yield: 6 cups (1.4 l) (6 servings)

1 garlic clove, peeled

1 1/2 pounds (680 g) ripe tomatoes, quartered, divided use

1/2 pound (227 g) cucumber, divided use

1/2 green bell pepper, quartered, divided use

2 scallions, white and light green parts only

1/4 jalapeño, seeded

2 teaspoons kosher salt

1/4 cup (15 g) flat leaf parsley

2 Tablespoons (11 g) fresh mint leaves

2 Tablespoons (30 ml) extra virgin olive oil

1 Tablespoon sherry vinegar

1 1/2 cups (360 ml) tomato juice

ground black pepper

1. Place garlic, half of the tomatoes, half of the cucumber, half of the bell pepper, half of scallions, and jalapeño into the Vitamix container and secure lid.

2. Select Variable 1.

3. Switch machine to Start and slowly increase speed to Variable 5.

4. Blend for 10 seconds. Remove to a large bowl.

5. Add all remaining ingredients into the Vitamix container and secure lid.

6. Select Variable 1.

7. Press Pulse 5 to 6 times. Increase speed to Variable 2 and continue Pulsing if desired to obtain finer consistency. Add to the gazpacho in large bowl. Chill for 1 to 2 hours before serving.

 nutritional information: *Amount Per Serving: Calories 90, Total Fat 5g, Saturated Fat 0.5g, Cholesterol 0mg, Sodium 840mg, Total Carbohydrates 10g, Dietary Fiber 2g, Protein 2g*

note: If you prefer a spicier soup, increase the amount of jalapeño and do not remove the seeds.

vegetarian *chili* with *cornbread crust*

preparation: 25 minutes plus overnight soaking • ***processing:*** 40 seconds plus Pulsing
cook time: 8 hours • ***yield:*** 8 servings

chili:

1 pound (454 g) dried black beans

4 cups (960 ml) water

6 allspice berries

1 teaspoon cumin seed

1 teaspoon coriander seed

1/4 teaspoon aniseed

1 stick cinnamon

28–ounce (794 g) can crushed tomatoes

1 medium onion,
4 1/2 ounces (128 g), chopped

3 garlic cloves, peeled

1/4 cup (38 g) chopped red bell pepper

1/4 cup (38 g) chopped green bell pepper

1 teaspoon dried oregano

1 Tablespoon chili powder

1 teaspoon salt

1/4 cup (22 g) cocoa powder

cornbread crust:

1 1/2 cups (183 g) whole grain cornmeal

1 cup (125 g) all-purpose flour

1/4 cup (50 g) granulated sugar

1 1/2 teaspoons baking powder

1/2 teaspoon baking soda

2 large eggs

2 Tablespoons (30 ml) vegetable oil

1 cup (240 ml) buttermilk

optional toppings:

1/2 cup (115 g) sour cream

1/4 cup (25 g) sliced scallions

1/2 cup (64 g) sliced black olives

1/2 cup (8 g) chopped fresh cilantro

1. Soak beans overnight in enough water to cover. Drain and rinse.

2. Place allspice, cumin seed, coriander seed, and aniseed into the Vitamix container and secure lid.

3. Select Variable 6.

4. Switch machine to Start and blend for 30 seconds.

5. Place soaked beans, 4 cups (960 ml) water, ground spices, cinnamon stick, tomatoes, onion, garlic, bell peppers, oregano, chili powder, salt, and cocoa powder into a 7-quart slow cooker. Cover and cook on High for 7 hours, or until the beans are tender.

6. To make cornbread crust: Place cornmeal, flour, sugar, baking powder, and baking soda into the Vitamix container and secure lid.

7. Select Variable 4.

8. Pulse 10 times. Remove lid and scrape sides. Pulse 2 more times so a hole forms in center of mixture. .

9. Remove lid and add eggs, oil, and buttermilk.

10. Pulse 5 times. Scrape down sides and repeat twice, or until all cornmeal is incorporated.

11. Spread cornbread mixture over top of the chili, and continue cooking 1 hour longer with lid off.

12. Ladle soup into bowls. Top each with optional ingredients if desired.

> **nutritional information:** *Amount Per Serving (with optional toppings): Calories 520, Total Fat 10g, Saturated Fat 2.5g, Cholesterol 60mg, Sodium 730mg, Total Carbohydrates 86g, Dietary Fiber 21g, Protein 22g*

note: Try adding 1/3 cup (38 g) shredded cheddar cheese to the cornbread when adding in the eggs, oil, and buttermilk.

broccoli cheese *soup*

preparation: 15 minutes • ***processing:*** 5 minutes 45 seconds • ***yield:*** 2 1/4 cups (540 ml) (2 servings)

1 cup (240 ml) milk

1/2 cup (56 g) shredded cheddar cheese

2 cups (312 g) steamed broccoli, divided use

1 teaspoon diced onion

1/2 chicken bouillon cube

1. Place milk, cheese, 1 1/2 cups broccoli, onion and bouillon into the Vitamix container in the order listed and secure lid.

2. Select Variable 1.

3. Switch machine to Start and slowly increase speed to Variable 10.

4. Blend for 5 minutes 45 seconds or until steam escapes from the vented lid.

5. Place 1/4 cup (39 g) steamed broccoli in each bowl. Pour soup over broccoli and serve.

>> **nutritional information:** *Amount Per Serving: Calories 250, Total Fat 14g, Saturated Fat 8g, Cholesterol 40mg, Sodium 530mg, Total Carbohydrate 18g, Dietary Fiber 5g, Protein 15g*

note: Steam and reserve an extra cup of broccoli or cauliflower florets to add to your finished soup when serving.

simple tomato *soup*

preparation: 15 minutes • **processing:** 6 minutes 15 seconds • **yield:** 4 3/4 cups (1.1 l) (4 servings)

2 14 1/2-ounce (410 g) cans diced tomatoes with herbs

1/2 small onion, 2 ounces (56 g), halved

1 small stalk celery, 2 ounces (56 g), halved

1 garlic clove, peeled

dash hot sauce

1/2 cup (120 m) half & half

salt and ground black pepper

1. Place tomatoes, onion, celery, garlic, and hot sauce into the Vitamix container and secure lid.

2. Select Variable 1.

3. Switch machine to Start and slowly increase speed to Variable 10.

4. Blend for 5 minutes 45 seconds.

5. Reduce speed to Variable 1 and remove the lid plug. Pour in half & half through the lid plug opening and replace lid plug.

6. Slowly increase speed to Variable 10. Blend for 30 seconds. Season to taste with salt and pepper.

>> **nutritional information:** *Amount Per Serving: Calories 110, Total Fat 3.5g, Saturated Fat 2g, Cholesterol 10mg, Sodium 570mg, Total Carbohydrates 16g, Dietary Fiber 2g, Protein 3g*

lemony leek *soup*

preparation: 25 minutes • **processing:** 30 - 45 seconds • **cook time:** 30 minutes
chill time: 2 hours • **yield:** 6 1/2 cups (1.5 l) (6 servings)

2 Tablespoons (30 ml) olive oil

6 1/2 cups (579 g) thinly sliced leeks, white and pale green parts only

4 ounces (114 g) Russet potato, quartered

4 cups (960 ml) chicken broth or vegetable broth

3 Tablespoons (9 g) fresh dill, divided use

1/4 teaspoon grated nutmeg

1/4 cup (60 g) plain yogurt

1 Tablespoon lemon zest

salt and ground black pepper

dill sprigs for garnish

1. Heat olive oil in a heavy large pot over medium heat. Add leeks and cook until softened and wilted, stirring often, 5 to 6 minutes.

2. Add potato, stir to coat. Add broth and bring to a boil. Reduce heat to medium and simmer until vegetables are tender, about 15 minutes. Take off heat and let cool 10 minutes.

3. Place mixture into the Vitamix container, add 2 Tablespoons dill, nutmeg and secure lid.

4. Select Variable 1.

5. Switch machine to Start and slowly increase speed to Variable 10.

6. Blend for 30 to 45 seconds.

7. Season to taste with salt and pepper. Cover and chill soup 2 hours.

8. Before serving, whisk lemon zest and 1 Tablespoon chopped dill into the plain yogurt. Season with salt and pepper.

9. Divide soup into 6 bowls and garnish with a Tablespoon of yogurt sauce.

 **nutritional information:** *Amount Per Serving: Calories 130, Total Fat 5g, Saturated Fat 0.5g, Cholesterol 5mg Sodium 680mg, Total Carbohydrates 19g, Dietary Fiber 2g, Protein 3g*

note: Soup is also delicious served hot.

garden fresh vegetable *soup*

preparation: 10 minutes • **processing:** 5 minutes 45 seconds • **yield:** 6 1/2 cups (1.5 l) (6 servings)

1 cup (240 ml) hot water

14-ounce (398 g) can diced tomatoes

10-ounce (284 g) box frozen spinach, thawed

1/2 medium cucumber (175 g), halved

1 medium carrot (80 g), halved

1 stalk celery (75 g), halved

1/3 cup (30 g) broccoli florets

1 vegetable bouillon cube

1 Tablespoon chopped fresh garlic (2 cloves)

5-6 thin slices (11 g) fresh ginger root

1/4 teaspoon dried sage

1/4 teaspoon ground cumin

1/4 teaspoon dried basil

dash of hot sauce

1. Place all ingredients into the Vitamix container in the order listed and secure lid.
2. Select Variable 1.
3. Switch machine to Start and slowly increase speed to Variable 10.
4. Blend for 5 minutes 45 seconds, using the tamper to press the ingredients into the blades.
5. Serve immediately.

>> **nutritional information:** *Amount Per Serving: Calories 45, Total Fat 0.5g, Saturated Fat 0g, Cholesterol 0mg, Sodium 360mg, Total Carbohydrates 9g, Dietary Fiber 3g, Protein 3g*

note: To quickly thaw spinach, remove foil cover and place on plate in microwave. Cook on High for 2 minutes.

tortilla *soup*

preparation: 15 minutes • *processing:* 5 minutes 10 seconds • *yield:* 2 1/2 cups (600 ml) (2 servings)

soup base:

1 cup (240 ml) chicken, beef or vegetable broth

1 Roma tomato, halved

1 medium carrot, halved

1 stalk celery, halved

1 thin slice onion

1 garlic clove, peeled

1 thin slice yellow squash

1 thin slice red bell pepper

1 thin slice cabbage

1 white mushroom

salt and ground black pepper to taste

1 teaspoon taco seasoning

dash cumin

optional ingredients:

1/2 cup (70 g) cooked chicken, chunked

1/2 fresh jalapeño

1/4 cup (30 g) sliced olives

1/4 cup (50 g) unsalted canned corn, drained

1 ounce (28 g) tortilla chips

1. Place all Soup Base ingredients into the Vitamix container in the order listed and secure lid.

2. Select Variable 1.

3. Switch machine to Start and slowly increase speed to Variable 10.

4. Blend for 5 minutes.

5. If adding optional ingredients, reduce speed to Variable 1. Remove lid plug.

6. Drop in chicken, jalapeños, olives, corn and chips through the lid plug opening.

7. Blend for an additional 10 seconds.

 **nutritional information:** *Amount Per Serving (with Optional Ingredients): Calories 260, Total Fat 11g, Saturated Fat 2g, Cholesterol 15mg, Sodium 530mg, Total Carbohydrates 32g, Dietary Fiber 4g, Protein 9g*

dressings & marinades

dressings & marinades

dressings • marinade • rubs

fresh apple and pear *dressing*

preparation: 15 minutes • ***processing:*** 15 seconds plus Pulsing • ***cook time:*** 30 minutes
yield: 2 1/4 cups (540 ml) (16 servings)

1 ripe pear, 8 ounces (227 g), cored, chopped

1 ripe apple, 8 ounces (227 g), cored, chopped

1/4 cup (50 g) granulated sugar

2/3 cup (160 ml) water

1 teaspoon fresh tarragon leaves or 2 teaspoons dried

2 Tablespoons (30 ml) apple cider vinegar

2 Tablespoons (30 ml) fresh lemon juice

1. Place fruit, sugar, water, and tarragon in a medium-size saucepan. Bring to a simmer, covered over medium heat, and cook until very soft, about 8 minutes.

2. Let water evaporate. There should be about 1 3/4 cups (420 ml) fruit and liquid when finished cooking. Allow the mixture to cool 15 minutes.

3. Pour mixture into the Vitamix container and secure lid.

4. Select Variable 1.

5. Switch machine to Start and slowly increase speed to Variable 10.

6. Blend for 20 seconds or until smooth.

7. Add apple cider vinegar and lemon juice to the Vitamix container and secure lid.

8. Select Variable 1.

9. Pulse 2 to 3 times to combine.

looking good

This fresh fruit dressing is perfect for mixed greens. Try adding a few pear slices, crumbled feta or blue cheese and crisp prosciutto for a light but satisfying lunch.

nutritional information: *Amount Per 2 Tablespoon (30 ml) Serving: Calories 30, Total Fat 0g, Saturated Fat 0g, Cholesterol 0mg, Sodium 0mg, Total Carbohydrate 8g, Dietary Fiber 1g, Protein 0g*

pineapple salad *dressing*

preparation: 15 minutes • **processing:** 15 seconds plus drizzle
yield: 2 1/2 cups (600 ml) (20 servings)

1/2 cup (120 ml) pineapple juice

4 ounces (114 g) pineapple chunks

1 lemon, peeled, halved

1/4 cup (60 ml) white vinegar

2 Tablespoons (30 ml) honey

1 cup (240 ml) olive oil

1. Place juice, pineapple, lemon, vinegar and honey into the Vitamix container in the order listed and secure lid.

2. Select Variable 1.

3. Switch machine to Start and slowly increase speed to Variable 7.

4. Blend for 15 seconds.

5. Reduce speed to Variable 3 and remove the lid plug. Slowly pour oil through the lid plug opening until emulsified and all of the oil is used up.

 nutritional information: *Amount Per 2 Tablespoon (30 ml) Serving: Calories 110, Total Fat 11g, Saturated Fat 1.5g, Cholesterol 0mg, Sodium 0mg, Total Carbohydrate 3g, Dietary Fiber 0g, Protein 0g*

note: Perfect on a fresh spinach and mixed greens salad topped with shredded coconut and toasted almonds.

citrus molasses
marinade

preparation: 25 minutes • **processing:** 20 seconds
yield: 1 cup (240 ml) (2 servings)

3/4 cup (180 ml) pineapple juice

2 Tablespoons (30 ml) pomegranate molasses
(see sidebar)

1 Tablespoon fresh lime juice

1 teaspoon lime zest

2 garlic cloves, peeled

1/2 teaspoon cumin seeds

2 teaspoons chopped cilantro leaves

1/2 jalapeño, 1/2 ounce (14 g), seeded

1. Place all ingredients into the Vitamix container in the order listed and secure lid.

2. Select Variable 1.

3. Switch machine to Start and slowly increase speed to Variable 7.

4. Blend for 20 seconds.

 nutritional information: *Amount Per Serving: Calories 80, Total Fat 0g, Saturated Fat 0g, Cholesterol 0mg, Sodium 10mg, Total Carbohydrate 18g, Dietary Fiber 0g, Protein 0g*

note: This is a great accompaniment to beef, pork, chicken, and tofu as a marinade, or brush on for grilling.

making pomegranate molasses

Pomegranate molasses is available in Middle Eastern and health food markets, but it's so easy to make at home. Place 4 cups (960 ml) pomegranate juice, 1/2 cup (100 g) granulated sugar, and 1 Tablespoon fresh lemon juice into a 4-quart saucepan and set over medium heat. Cook, stirring occasionally until the sugar is completely dissolved. Reduce heat to medium-low and cook until the mixture has reduced to 1 cup, about 1 1/2 hours. It should be the consistency of thick syrup. Remove saucepan from the heat and allow to cool for 30 minutes. Transfer to a glass jar and allow to cool completely before using or covering and storing in the refrigerator for up to 4 months. You can use pomegranate molasses in beverages, sauces, marinades, salad dressings, and many other dishes.

raspberry maple *dressing*

preparation: 10 minutes • ***processing:*** 30 seconds • ***yield:*** 2 1/2 cups (600 ml) (20 servings)

1 cup (240 ml) raspberry vinegar (see sidebar)

4 Tablespoons (60 ml) maple syrup

pinch of salt

pinch of ground black pepper

1 1/4 cups (300 ml) olive oil

1. Place vinegar, maple syrup, salt and pepper into the Vitamix container in the order listed and secure lid.

2. Select Variable 1.

3. Switch machine to Start and slowly increase speed to Variable 7.

4. Remove the lid plug and slowly pour olive oil through the lid plug opening.

5. Once all the oil is incorporated, slowly increase speed to Variable 10.

6. Blend for 10 seconds.

 nutritional information: *Amount Per 2 Tablespoon (30 ml) Serving: Calories 140, Total Fat 14g, Saturated Fat 2g, Cholesterol 0mg, Sodium 0mg, Total Carbohydrate 4g, Dietary Fiber 0g, Protein 0g*

homemade vinegars

Here's a simple way to create colorful, healthy, delicious vinegars perfect for any gift-giving occasion. Fill a pint jar with freshly washed red raspberries, packing the raspberries to fill the jar. Pour apple cider vinegar over the raspberries, being sure to cover them completely. Cover the jar securely with plastic wrap and place on a sunny windowsill for 4 to 6 weeks. Strain the liquid through cheesecloth or a very fine mesh strainer; discard the raspberries. Pour raspberry vinegar into a decorative bottle and store in a cool, dry cabinet. Friends and relatives will enjoy tossing this light raspberry vinegar with a salmon salad, using it as a marinade, or incorporating it into other recipes.

creamy avocado *dressing*

preparation: 15 minutes • ***processing:*** 20 seconds • ***yield:*** 1 1/4 cups (300 ml) (10 servings)

1/4 cup (60 ml) 2% milk

1/2 cup (120 g) reduced fat sour cream

1/4 cup (56 g) light mayonnaise

1 Tablespoon fresh lemon juice

1 large ripe avocado, 9 ounces (256 g), peeled, pitted

2-3 drops hot pepper sauce

1/8-1/4 teaspoon garlic powder

1/2 teaspoon salt

1/4 teaspoon ground white pepper

1. Place all ingredients into the Vitamix container in the order listed and secure lid.

2. Select Variable 1.

3. Switch machine to Start and slowly increase speed to Variable 10.

4. Blend for 20 seconds.

 nutritional information: *Amount Per 2 Tablespoon (30 ml) Serving: Calories 90, Total Fat 8g, Saturated Fat 2g, Cholesterol 10mg, Sodium 170mg, Total Carbohydrate 4g, Dietary Fiber 2g, Protein 1g*

basic vinaigrette *dressing*

preparation: 10 minutes • **processing:** 20 seconds plus drizzle
yield: 2 1/4 cups (540 ml) (18 servings)

1/2 cup (120 ml) red wine vinegar

2 teaspoons Dijon mustard

1/2 teaspoon ground black pepper

1/2-1 teaspoon kosher salt

1 1/2 cups (360 ml) olive oil

1/2 cup (10 g) fresh herb blend

1. Place vinegar, Dijon, pepper and salt into the Vitamix container in the order listed and secure lid.

2. Select Variable 1.

3. Switch machine to Start and slowly increase speed to Variable 3.

4. Blend for 10 seconds. Remove the lid plug and slowly drizzle oil through the lid plug opening. Once oil is incorporated, add the herbs through the lid plug opening and blend for 10 seconds.

>> **nutritional information:** *Amount Per 2 Tablespoon (30 ml) Serving: Calories 160, Total Fat 18g, Saturated Fat 2.5g, Cholesterol 0mg, Sodium 70mg, Total Carbohydrate 0g, Dietary Fiber 0g, Protein 0g*

note: Try oregano, sage, and dill for a fresh herb blend, but any blend will work. Refrigerate in an airtight container for up to 2 weeks.

orange vanilla vinaigrette *dressing*

preparation: 15 minutes • **processing:** 30 seconds • **yield:** 3 cups (720 ml) (24 servings)

2 oranges, peeled, halved

1 Tablespoon apple cider vinegar

1 1/2 teaspoons vanilla extract

1 Tablespoon honey

1 lemon, peeled, halved

1 dash hot sauce

1/4 teaspoon salt

1/8 teaspoon ground black pepper

1 1/2 cups (360 ml) extra virgin olive oil

1. Place oranges, vinegar, vanilla, honey, lemon, hot sauce, salt and pepper into the Vitamix container in the order listed and secure lid.

2. Select Variable 1.

3. Switch machine to Start and slowly increase speed to Variable 6.

4. Blend for 20 seconds or until smooth. Reduce speed to Variable 1 and remove the lid plug.

5. Slowly pour olive oil through the lid plug opening until emulsified.

6. Serve over spinach salad with mandarin oranges.

 **nutritional information:** *Amount Per 2 Tablespoon (30 ml) Serving: Calories 140, Total Fat 14g, Saturated Fat 2g, Cholesterol 0mg, Sodium 25mg, Total Carbohydrate 2g, Dietary Fiber 0g, Protein 0g*

bright idea

Salad dressings make wonderful marinades for fish or poultry. You can also brush a salad dressing on fish or poultry during grilling.

carrot ginger vinaigrette *dressing*

preparation: 15 minutes • ***processing:*** 20 seconds • ***yield:*** 1 1/2 cups (360 ml) (12 servings)

1 medium carrot, 4 ounces (114 g), rough chopped

1 cup (240 ml) water

1/4 cup (60 ml) rice vinegar

2 teaspoons fresh lemon juice

4 teaspoons low sodium soy sauce

4 teaspoons sesame oil

1/4 teaspoon salt

2 teaspoons packed light brown sugar

2 Tablespoons (12 g) chopped peeled fresh ginger root

1. Place carrot and water in a small saucepan. Bring to a simmer over medium-low heat and cook until tender, about 15 minutes. Reserve 1/2 cup (120 ml) cooking liquid, and then drain the carrot.

2. Place carrots, cooking liquid, vinegar, lemon juice, soy sauce, sesame oil, salt, brown sugar and ginger and into the Vitamix container in the order listed and secure lid.

3. Select Variable 1.

4. Switch machine to Start and slowly increase speed to Variable 7.

5. Blend for 20 seconds. Chill thoroughly before serving.

>> ***nutritional information:*** *Amount Per 2 Tablespoon (30 ml) Serving: Calories 25, Total Fat 1.5g, Saturated Fat 0g, Cholesterol 0mg, Sodium 180mg, Total Carbohydrate 3g, Dietary Fiber 0g, Protein 0g*

light ranch *dressing*

preparation: 15 minutes • **processing:** 15-20 seconds • **yield:** 2 1/4 cups (540 ml) (18 servings)

1 1/3 cups (320 ml) low-fat buttermilk

1/2 cup (120 g) light mayonnaise

4 teaspoons Worcestershire sauce

1 teaspoon onion powder

1 teaspoon dried onion flakes

1/2 teaspoon garlic powder

2 Tablespoon (6 g) fresh chives

2 Tablespoons (1 g) fresh dill

2 Tablespoons (8 g) fresh parsley leaves

1. Place all ingredients into the Vitamix container in the order listed and secure lid.

2. Select Variable 1.

3. Switch machine to Start and slowly increase speed to Variable 6.

4. Blend for 15 to 20 seconds.

 nutritional information: *Amount Per 2 Tablespoon (30 ml) Serving: Calories 30, Total Fat 2.5g, Saturated Fat 0g, Cholesterol 5mg, Sodium 75mg, Total Carbohydrate 2g, Dietary Fiber 0g, Protein 1g*

note: Be careful not to overdo it when pouring this dressing on salad. Because it has a thinner consistency than storebought Ranch dressing, a little goes a long way. Refrigerate in an airtight container for three to four days.

caesar salad *dressing*

preparation: 15 minutes • *processing:* 35 seconds • *yield:* 4 cups (960 ml) (32 servings)

6 large eggs

2 Tablespoons (30 ml) red wine vinegar

1/2 cup plus 1 Tablespoon (135 ml) fresh lemon juice

1 1/2 small garlic cloves, peeled

1 cup (100 g) grated Parmesan cheese

1/2 teaspoon salt

1 Tablespoon plus 1 1/2 teaspoons anchovy filets

1/3 teaspoon dry mustard

1 cup plus 2 Tablespoons (270 ml) extra virgin olive oil

1. Place eggs, vinegar, lemon juice, garlic, cheese, salt, anchovy and mustard into the Vitamix container in the order listed and secure lid.

2. Select Variable 1.

3. Switch machine to Start and slowly increase speed to Variable 7.

4. Blend for 25 seconds or until smooth. Reduce speed to Variable 2 and remove the lid plug.

5. Slowly pour olive oil through the lid plug opening and blend an additional 10 seconds.

>> **nutritional information:** *Amount Per 2 Tablespoon (30 ml) Serving: Calories 100, Total Fat 10g, Saturated Fat 2g, Cholesterol 40mg, Sodium 115mg, Total Carbohydrate 1g, Dietary Fiber 0g, Protein 2g*

note: Refrigerate in an airtight container for three to four days.

light italian *dressing*

preparation: 15 minutes • *processing:* 20 seconds • *yield:* 1 1/2 cups (360 ml) (12 servings)

1 medium tomato, 3 1/2 ounces (100 g), halved

2 Tablespoons (30 ml) red wine vinegar

2 Tablespoons (30 ml) fresh lemon juice

1/2 cup (120 ml) water

4 teaspoons Dijon mustard

1/8 teaspoon granulated sugar

2 Tablespoons (30 ml) extra virgin olive oil

1 garlic clove, peeled

1/4 teaspoon dried oregano

1/4 teaspoon dried basil

1/8 teaspoon kosher salt

ground black pepper to taste

1. Place all ingredients into the Vitamix container in the order listed and secure lid.

2. Select Variable 1.

3. Switch machine to Start and slowly increase speed to Variable 6.

4. Blend for 20 seconds.

 *nutritional information:* Amount Per 2 Tablespoon (30 ml) Serving: Calories 25, Total Fat 2.5g, Saturated Fat 0g, Cholesterol 0mg, Sodium 60mg, Total Carbohydrate 1g, Dietary Fiber 0g, Protein 0g

note: Refrigerate in an airtight container for up to 2 weeks.

spicy thousand island *dressing*

preparation: 20 minutes • ***processing:*** 15-20 seconds • ***yield:*** 2 1/4 cups (540 ml) (16 servings)

1 cup (245 g) low-fat plain yogurt

1/4 cup (60 g) mayonnaise

1/4 cup (68 g) ketchup

4 teaspoons Worcestershire sauce

6 Tablespoons (90 g) sweet pickle relish

6 Tablespoons (56 g) chopped red bell pepper

1 chipotle pepper in adobo sauce

1/2 teaspoon kosher salt

1. Place all ingredients into the Vitamix container in the order listed and secure lid.

2. Select Variable 1.

3. Switch machine to Start and slowly increase speed to Variable 3.

4. Blend for 15 to 20 seconds.

 nutritional information: *Amount Per 2 Tablespoon (30 ml) Serving: Calories 50, Total Fat 3g, Saturated Fat 0.5g, Cholesterol 0mg, Sodium 200mg, Total Carbohydrate 5g, Dietary Fiber 0g, Protein 1g*

note: Refrigerate in an airtight container for up to 2 weeks.

raspberry vinaigrette *dressing*

preparation: 10 minutes • ***processing:*** 20-30 seconds • ***yield:*** 1 3/4 cups (420 ml) (14 servings)

3/4 cup (180 ml) olive oil

1/4 cup (60 ml) apple cider or raspberry vinegar

1 teaspoon salt

1 teaspoon dried basil

1/2 cup (60 g) fresh or frozen red raspberries

1/4 cup (60 ml) water

2 Tablespoons (30 ml) honey

1. Place olive oil, vinegar, salt, basil, raspberries and water into the Vitamix container in the order listed and secure lid.

2. Select Variable 1.

3. Switch machine to Start and remove the lid plug. Add honey through the lid plug opening and replace lid plug.

4. Slowly increase speed to Variable 6.

5. Blend for 20 to 30 seconds.

 **nutritional information:** *Amount Per 2 Tablespoon (30 ml) Serving: Calories 120, Total Fat 12g, Saturated Fat 1.5g, Cholesterol 0mg, Sodium 170mg, Total Carbohydrate 4g, Dietary Fiber 0g, Protein 0g*

note: Refrigerate in an airtight container for up to 2 weeks.

balsamic citrus *dressing*

preparation: 10 minutes • **processing:** 20 seconds plus drizzle
yield: 2 1/2 cups (600 ml) (20 servings)

1/4 cup (60 ml) balsamic vinegar

2 Tablespoons (30 ml) fresh lime juice

3 medium oranges, peeled, halved

3 green onion, white part only

2 garlic cloves, peeled

2 Tablespoons (25 g) granulated sugar

1/8 teaspoon ground white pepper

1 teaspoon kosher salt

1/2 cup (120 ml) extra virgin olive oil

1. Place vinegar, lime juice, oranges, onion, garlic, sugar, white pepper and salt into the Vitamix container in the order listed and secure lid.

2. Select Variable 1.

3. Switch machine to Start and slowly increase speed to Variable 7.

4. Blend for 20 seconds. Reduce speed to Variable 2 and remove the lid plug. Slowly pour oil through the lid plug opening until emulsified.

 **nutritional information:** *Amount Per 2 Tablespoon (30 ml) Serving: Calories 70, Total Fat 6g, Saturated Fat 1g, Cholesterol 0mg, Sodium 95mg, Total Carbohydrate 5g, Dietary Fiber 1g, Protein 0g*

spanish spice *rub*

preparation: 10 minutes • ***processing:*** 15 seconds • ***yield:*** 1/2 cup (120 g) (8 servings)

6 Tablespoons (41 g) Spanish paprika

1 Tablespoon cumin seeds

1 Tablespoon fennel seeds

2 teaspoons kosher salt

1 teaspoon whole peppercorns

1. Place all ingredients into the Vitamix container and secure lid.

2. Select Variable 1.

3. Switch machine to Start and slowly increase speed to Variable 7.

4. Blend for 15 seconds.

 nutritional information: *Amount Per 1 Tablespoon Serving: Calories 20, Total Fat 1g, Saturated Fat 0g, Cholesterol 0mg, Sodium 490mg, Total Carbohydrate 4g, Dietary Fiber 2g, Protein 1g*

jerk *seasoning*

preparation: 10 minutes • **processing:** 13 seconds
yield: 3/4 cup (180 g) (12 servings)

3 Tablespoons (30 g) whole allspice berries

1 Tablespoon black peppercorns

2 teaspoons whole cloves

2 teaspoons crushed red pepper flakes

1 Tablespoon dried thyme leaves

1 Tablespoon salt

1 teaspoon ground cinnamon

1/4 cup (55 g) firmly packed brown sugar

1. Place allspice, peppercorns, cloves and pepper flakes into the Vitamix container and secure lid.

2. Select Variable 1.

3. Switch machine to Start and slowly increase speed to Variable 4.

4. Blend for 10 seconds or until mixture is a medium-fine powder. Add remaining ingredients and secure lid.

5. Select Variable 1.

6. Switch machine to Start and slowly increase speed to Variable 3.

7. Blend for 3 seconds.

8. Store in covered container at room temperature. Use as a rub on grilled pork, shrimp or chicken, or any Jamaican-influenced recipe.

 nutritional information: *Amount Per 1 Tablespoon Serving: Calories 20, Total Fat 0g, Saturated Fat 0g, Cholesterol 0mg, Sodium 580mg, Total Carbohydrate 5g, Dietary Fiber 0g, Protein 0g*

kitchen prep

Brush strip steak with olive oil, and rub both sides with Spanish Spice Rub. Grill 3 to 4 minutes over high heat on each side for medium rare doneness.

note: Grinding herbs on a regular basis releases volatile oils that may cause your container to discolor or emit a lingering odor.

salads & sides

grains

salads

coleslaws

vegetables

salads & sides

coleslaws • grains • salads • vegetables

cornbread

---

preparation: 15 minutes • ***processing:*** 1 minute 15 seconds • ***bake time:*** 20 minutes
yield: 12 slices

2 cups (416 g) popcorn kernels

1 cup (125 g) all-purpose flour

1/2 cup (100 g) granulated sugar

1 Tablespoon baking powder

1/2 teaspoon salt

1/4 cup (56 g) unsalted butter

1 cup (240 ml) milk

1 large egg

1. Heat oven to 400°F (200°C). Spray the bottom and sides of an 8–inch (20 cm) square pan with cooking spray or olive oil.

2. Place popcorn kernels into the Vitamix container and secure lid.

3. Select Variable 1.

4. Switch machine to Start and slowly increase speed to Variable 10.

5. Blend for 1 minute. Measure out 1 1/4 cups (153 g) and place into a medium-sized mixing bowl. Add flour, sugar, baking powder and salt. Mix lightly by hand and set aside. Place left over cornmeal into a sealed container and store in a cool dry place.

6. Place butter, milk and egg into the Vitamix container and secure lid.

7. Select Variable 1.

8. Switch machine to Start and slowly increase speed to Variable 5.

9. Blend for 15 seconds.

10. Pour into dry mixture and mix by hand until flour is moistened. Spread batter into prepared baking pan.

11. Bake 20 minutes or until toothpick inserted into center comes out clean.

>> **nutritional information:** *Amount Per Slice: Calories 120, Total Fat 5g, Saturated Fat 3g, Cholesterol 30mg, Sodium 230mg, Total Carbohydrate 18g, Fiber 0g, Protein 2g*

note: Use leftovers for cauliflower gratin recipe found in this section.

cauliflower *gratin*

preparation: 25 minutes • **processing:** 35–40 seconds • **cook time:** 15 minutes
bake time: 25 minutes • **yield:** 7 servings

4 Tablespoons (56 g) butter, divided use

1 cup (160 g) chopped shallots

9 cups (900 g) cauliflower florets

1 1/4 cups (300 ml) chicken broth

3/4 cup (180 ml) heavy cream

1 teaspoon plus 1 Tablespoon Dijon mustard

1 teaspoon plus 1 Tablespoon chopped fresh sage

1 Tablespoon all-purpose flour

1–inch x 1/2–inch (2.5 cm x 1.3 cm) slice lemon peel

1 1/2 cups (300 g) crumbled Cornbread

1. Preheat oven to 375°F (190°C). Melt 2 Tablespoons (28 g) butter in a large pot over medium-high heat. Add shallots and sauté 4 minutes. Add cauliflower, season with salt and pepper, and then add broth. Cover and steam until cauliflower is tender, 10 minutes.

2. Transfer cauliflower to a bowl with a slotted spoon. Place remaining liquid and shallots into the Vitamix container. Add heavy cream, 1 teaspoon mustard, 1 teaspoon fresh sage, flour, lemon peel, and secure lid.

3. Select Variable 1.

4. Switch machine to Start and slowly increase speed to Variable 10.

5. Blend for 35 to 40 seconds.

6. Arrange cauliflower stem side down in a 9–inch (23 cm) square pan. Pour sauce over top.

7. Melt 2 Tablespoons (28 g) butter in a medium skillet over medium heat. Whisk in 1 Tablespoon mustard and 1 Tablespoon fresh sage. Add cornbread crumbs and toss to coat. Spread over cauliflower. Bake for 25 minutes or until top is golden.

>> **nutritional information:** *Amount Per Serving: Calories 320, Total Fat 21g, Saturated Fat 13g, Cholesterol 80mg, Sodium 560mg, Total Carbohydrate 29g, Fiber 4g, Protein 6g*

note: Peel the lemon using a vegetable peeler to ensure just the peel and not the bitter pith makes it into the recipe.

sautéed
brussels *sprouts*

preparation: 10 minutes • **processing:** Pulsing
cook time: 15 minutes • **yield:** 4 servings

1 pound (454 g) Brussels sprouts, trimmed

3 Tablespoons (42 g) butter, divided use

3 ounces (85 g) shallots, thinly sliced

2 Tablespoons (30 ml) apple cider vinegar

1 Tablespoon granulated sugar

1/2 cup (120 ml) water

1. Place Brussels sprouts into the Vitamix container, fill with water to the 6 cup (1.4 l) mark and secure lid.

2. Select Variable 8.

3. Pulse 6 times until sprouts are shredded. Drain and set aside.

4. Melt 2 Tablespoons (28 g) butter over medium heat in a large fry pan. Add shallots and sauté 3 minutes. Add cider vinegar and sugar; cook 2 minutes, stirring frequently. Remove to a plate.

5. Add remaining Tablespoon of butter and increase heat to medium high. Add Brussels sprouts, salt, pepper to taste, and cook 5 minutes. Add water and cook 5 more minutes. Stir in cooked shallots.

 nutritional information: *Amount Per Serving: Calories 150, Total Fat 9g, Saturated Fat 6g, Cholesterol 25mg, Sodium 105mg, Total Carbohydrate 18g, Dietary Fiber 4g, Protein 5g*

trimming brussels sprouts

Brussels sprouts can be an intimidating ingredient, but they're actually quite easy to prepare. First, trim the base of the sprout where it was attached to the stock as this becomes dry and tough during storage. Next, remove outer leaves that are thick or damaged until you're left with a nice tight sprout. Third, trim off a bit more of the core so you get a base where the leaves roughly start. Finally, if you're grilling or sautéing the sprouts, use your knife to slice a shallow X into the base to help it cook more evenly.

quinoa mango *salad*

preparation: 20 minutes • **processing:** 20–30 seconds • **cook time:** 15 minutes
yield: 10 cups (2.8 kg) salad (10 servings)

1 cup (170 g) uncooked quinoa, rinsed

4 cups (748 g) frozen mango chunks,
partially thawed, drained, divided use

1 cup (145 g) golden raisins

1/2 cup (50 g) sliced celery (1 stalk)

1/4 cup (40 g) diced red onion

1/2 cup (46 g) sliced almonds, toasted

1/2 cup (121 g) reduced fat sour cream

2 Tablespoons (30 ml) white
balsamic vinegar

2 teaspoons curry powder

1 teaspoon garlic salt

1 teaspoon ground black pepper

1. Heat 2 cups (480 ml) of water to a boil. Stir in quinoa and bring to a boil. Cover and reduce heat to simmer. Cook for 12 minutes or until quinoa absorbs almost all of the water. Fluff with a fork and let cool for 15 minutes.

2. Combine quinoa, 2 cups (374 g) mango, raisins, celery, red onion, and sliced almonds in a large bowl. Set aside.

3. Place 2 cups (374 g) thawed mango, sour cream, vinegar, curry, garlic salt and black pepper into the Vitamix container and secure lid.

4. Select Variable 1.

5. Switch machine to Start and slowly increase speed to Variable 7.

6. Blend for 20 to 30 seconds.

7. Pour over quinoa mixture to taste and toss to blend. Store extra dressing in the refrigerator.

>> **nutritional information:** *Amount Per Serving: Calories 210, Total Fat 5g, Saturated Fat 1g, Cholesterol 5mg, Sodium 105mg, Total Carbohydrate 39g, Dietary Fiber 4g, Protein 5g*

curried vegetable *salad*

preparation: 20 minutes • **processing:** 20 – 30 seconds plus Pulsing • **yield:** 4 servings

1 small carrot, 2 ounces (56 g), cut into 3 pieces

1 stalk celery, 2 ounces (56 g), cut into 3 pieces

1 medium red bell pepper, 9 ounces (255 g), seeded, quartered

1 medium green bell pepper, 7 ounces (200 g), seeded, quartered

1 scallion, diced

12 ounce (340 g) English cucumber, medium diced

6 Tablespoons (90 ml) apple cider vinegar

2 teaspoons Dijon mustard

2 teaspoons fresh lemon juice

1 ounce (28 g) red onion slice

1/2 teaspoon chopped garlic

2 teaspoons curry powder

1 teaspoon granulated sugar

1/8 teaspoon salt

1/2 cup (120 ml) olive oil

1. Place carrots and celery into the Vitamix container and secure lid.

2. Select Variable 6.

3. Pulse 7 or 8 times to chop. Remove to a large bowl.

4. Place peppers into the Vitamix container and secure lid.

5. Select Variable 5.

6. Pulse 3 times. Stop and scrape down sides of container. Pulse 2 more times. Remove to bowl. Add chopped cucumber and scallions to bowl and set aside.

7. Place vinegar, mustard, lemon juice, onion, garlic, curry, sugar, salt and olive oil into the Vitamix container and secure lid.

8. Select Variable 1.

9. Switch machine to Start and slowly increase speed to Variable 10. Blend for 20 to 30 seconds.

10. Before pouring dressing over salad, drain any extra liquid from chopped vegetables. Toss with salad dressing and serve.

>> **nutritional information:** *Amount Per Serving: Calories 310, Total Fat 28g, Saturated Fat 4g, Cholesterol 0mg, Sodium 180mg, Total Carbohydrate 14g, Dietary Fiber 4g, Protein 2g*

cranberry pecan *salad*

preparation: 15 minutes • **processing:** 20 seconds • **yield:** 4 servings using 1/2 cup (120 ml) dressing

3/4 cup (180 ml) cranberry juice

6 Tablespoons (90 g) Dijon mustard

6 Tablespoons (90 ml) canola oil

6 Tablespoons (90 ml) walnut oil

1 ounce (28 g) shallot

4 cups (80 g) arugula

2/3 cup (80 g) dried cranberries

1/3 cup (36 g) chopped pecans, toasted

1. Place juice, mustard, oils and shallot into the Vitamix container and secure lid.

2. Select Variable 1.

3. Switch machine to Start and slowly increase speed to Variable 7.

4. Blend for 20 seconds.

5. Toss 1/2 cup (120 ml) dressing with arugula, cranberries, and pecans.

6. Refrigerate remaining dressing. Dressing will keep for 1 to 2 weeks.

nutritional information: *Amount Per Serving: Calories 230, Total Fat 17g, Saturated Fat 1.5g, Cholesterol 0mg, Sodium 140mg, Total Carbohydrate 21g, Dietary Fiber 2g, Protein 1g*

bright idea

To get a deeper flavor from the pecans, toast them over medium heat in a dry skillet. Toss or stir frequently to prevent burning. Toast just until fragrant and remove from heat.

coconut milk, curry and chili paste with roasted *vegetables*

preparation: 20 minutes · **processing:** 5 minutes · **bake time:** 25–30 minutes
yield: 6 servings

vegetables:

1 pound (454 g) fingerling potatoes, washed, cut into 2–inch (5 cm) pieces

2 cups (200 g) cauliflower pieces, trimmed

2 cups (220 g) green beans, trimmed

1 1/2 cups (240 g) yellow onion, cut into wedges

1/4 cup (60 ml) vegetable oil

1/2 teaspoon salt

1/4 teaspoon freshly cracked black pepper

sauce:

2/3 cup (160 ml) light coconut milk

1 teaspoon roasted chile paste

1/4 teaspoon curry powder

1/4 teaspoon salt

1/8 teaspoon freshly cracked black pepper

1. Preheat oven to 400°F (200°C). In a 13–inch x 9–inch (33 cm x 23 cm) baking pan stir together all vegetable ingredients.

2. Bake for 25 to 30 minutes, stirring occasionally, until potatoes are tender. Remove from oven; keep warm.

3. Meanwhile, place all sauce ingredients into the Vitamix container and secure lid.

4. Select Variable 1.

5. Switch machine to Start and slowly increase speed to Variable 10.

6. Blend for 5 minutes or until sauce is hot.

7. Pour hot sauce over vegetables; mix well.

>> **nutritional information:** *Amount Per Serving: Calories 190, Total Fat 11g, Saturated Fat 2.5g, Cholesterol 0mg, Sodium 550mg, Total Carbohydrate 22g, Dietary Fiber 4g, Protein 3g*

polenta flax *cakes*
with rustic tomato *sauce*

preparation: 20 minutes • **processing:** 1 minute plus Pulsing • **cook time:** 1 hour
yield: 18 slices and 3 cups (720 ml) sauce (9 servings)

2 cups (416 g) popcorn kernels or 1 cup (122 g) whole grain cornmeal

4 cups (960 ml) water, divided use

1 teaspoon salt

1/3 cup (34 g) flax seed meal

1/4 cup (15 g) fresh parsley leaves

1/4 cup (25 g) grated Parmesan cheese

1 teaspoon whole flaxseed

2 Tablespoons (30 ml) olive oil

2 pounds (908 g) ripe tomatoes, quartered (approximately 6 tomatoes)

1. If starting with whole popcorn kernels, place 2 cups (480 g) into the Vitamix container and secure lid.

2. Select Variable 1.

3. Switch machine to Start and slowly increase speed to Variable 10.

4. Blend for 1 minute. Measure out 1 cup (122 g) and combine with 1 cup (240 ml) water. Place left over cornmeal into a sealed container and store in a cool dry place.

5. Bring 3 cups (720 ml) water to a boil. Add cornmeal and salt, stirring constantly until thickened, 2 minutes. Cover, reduce heat to low, and cook 10 minutes longer, stirring occasionally.

6. Remove from heat, stir in flaxseed meal, parsley, and parmesan cheese. Spoon into a 9-inch x 5-inch (23 cm x 13 cm) loaf pan. Sprinkle with whole flaxseed and chill for 2 hours.

7. Place 6 tomato quarters into the Vitamix machine and secure lid.

8. Select Variable 5.

9. Pulse 6 times. Pour out into a bowl and repeat with remaining tomato quarters.

10. Heat olive oil in a medium pan and add chopped tomatoes. Cook until tomatoes are soft and sauce has thickened, about 12 to 15 minutes.

11. When polenta is chilled, turn out onto cutting board and cut into 1/2-inch (1.3 cm) slices. Heat a lightly oiled nonstick pan over medium heat. Cook 4 polenta slices at a time, about 5 minutes on each side until golden brown. Keep warm until all slices are cooked.

12. Serve with warm tomato sauce.

>> **nutritional information:** *Amount Per Serving (2 Slices Polenta with 1/3 Cup (80 g) Sauce): Calories 120, Total Fat 6g, Saturated Fat 1g, Cholesterol 0mg, Sodium 310mg, Total Carbohydrate 16g, Dietary Fiber 4g, Protein 4g*

whole grain saffron *polenta*

preparation: 20 minutes • **processing:** 1 minute plus Pulsing • **cook time:** 35 minutes
yield: 4 servings

2 cups (416 g) popcorn kernels or 1 cup (122 g) polenta (coarse cornmeal)

2 Tablespoons (30 ml) olive oil

1 cup (160 g) chopped onion

4 cups (960 ml) reduced sodium chicken broth

3/4 teaspoon kosher salt

1/2 teaspoon saffron threads

1 1/2 cups (246 g) frozen corn kernels, thawed

1. If starting with whole popcorn kernels, place 2 cups (480 g) into the Vitamix container and secure lid.

2. Select Variable 1.

3. Switch machine to Start and slowly increase speed to Variable 10.

4. Blend for 1 minute. Measure out 1 cup (122 g). Place left over cornmeal into a sealed container and store in a cool dry place.

5. Heat oil in a large saucepan over medium-low heat. Add onion; cover and cook 5 to 8 minutes.

6. Add broth, salt and saffron. Bring to a boil then add in polenta. Cook, whisking constantly until it boils and starts to thicken, 2 to 3 minutes. Reduce heat to low. Simmer 10 minutes, stirring occasionally. Cover; simmer until cooked through and very thick, about 10 minutes longer.

7. Place thawed corn kernels into the Vitamix container and secure lid.

8. Select Variable 2.

9. Pulse 4 times. Remove lid, scrape down sides of container, and replace lid. Pulse 2 more times.

10. Stir into cooked polenta. Season to taste with salt and pepper if necessary.

nutritional information: *Amount Per Serving: Calories 290, Total Fat 7g, Saturated Fat 1g, Cholesterol 0mg, Sodium 810mg, Total Carbohydrate 49g, Fiber 6g, Protein 7g*

green *coleslaw*

preparation: 15 minutes • *processing:* Pulsing • *cook time:* 5 minutes
chill time: 4 hours – overnight • *yield:* 6 servings

1/2 pound (227 g) collard greens, tough stems removed, each leaf cut into quarters

1 large bell pepper, 9 ounce (256 g), any color, quartered

1 medium onion, 5 ounces (142 g), quartered

3 medium carrots, 9 1/2 ounces (270 g), cut into thirds

1/2 cup (120 ml) apple cider vinegar

1/3 cup (67 g) granulated sugar

1/4 cup (60 ml) canola oil

1 teaspoon dry mustard

1 teaspoon celery seed

1/2 teaspoon salt

1/4 teaspoon ground black pepper

1. Place half of the collard leaves into the Vitamix container, fill to 6 cup (1.4 l) mark with water, and secure lid.

2. Select Variable 5.

3. Pulse 3 times until chopped. Pour out into a colander and place in large-size mixing bowl. Repeat with remaining collard leaves.

4. Place pepper and onion quarters into the Vitamix container and secure lid.

5. Select Variable 5.

6. Pulse 6 to 7 times until chopped. Remove to bowl with chopped collards.

7. Place carrots into the Vitamix container and secure lid.

8. Select Variable 6.

9. Pulse 5 to 6 times until chopped. Remove to bowl containing other vegetables.

10. Add vinegar, sugar, oil, dry mustard, celery seed, salt and pepper to a small saucepan and stir together. Bring to a boil, stirring to dissolve sugar. Remove from heat and pour over collard and vegetable mixture. Stir to coat. For best result, cover and chill 4 hours or overnight before serving.

 **nutritional information:** *Amount Per Serving: Calories 170, Total Fat 10g, Saturated Fat 0.5g, Cholesterol 0mg, Sodium 240mg, Total Carbohydrate 22g, Dietary Fiber 4g, Protein 2g*

trimming collard greens

To prepare collard greens, lay each leaf flat on a cutting board. Use a sharp paring knife to cut along either side of the center spine, separating the entire leaf from the spine. To save time, you can also fold the leaf in half, so only one cut is necessary along the spine. If children are helping out in the kitchen, have them simply pull leaves away from the stem with their hands...a less precise, but certainly a practical technique.

sweet potato *pancakes*

preparation: 20 minutes • **processing:** Pulsing • **cook time:** 15 minutes
yield: 20 mini pancakes (5 servings)

1/3 cup (40 g) whole wheat flour

1/4 cup (26 g) flax seed meal

1 teaspoon baking powder

1/2 teaspoon salt

1/2 teaspoon curry powder

1/4 cup (60 ml) 2% milk

2 Tablespoons (30 ml) melted butter

1 large egg

2 Tablespoons (20 g) chopped onion

2 Tablespoons (2 g) cilantro leaves

2 cups (266 g) peeled sweet potato, rough chopped

2 teaspoons vegetable oil

1. In a large bowl, combine flour, flaxseed meal, baking powder, salt and curry powder. Stir by hand to combine. Set aside.

2. Place milk, melted butter, egg, onion, cilantro and sweet potato chunks into the Vitamix container and secure lid.

3. Select Variable 10.

4. Pulse 8 times or until sweet potato looks grated. Pour into dry mixture and mix by hand until combined.

5. Heat oil in a nonstick skillet over medium heat. Drop batter by rounded Tablespoons. Flatten slightly with back of the spoon. Cook 1 1/2 minutes or until browned. Flip over and gently press down with spatula. Cook an additional 1 1/2 minutes or until cooked through.

 nutritional information: *Amount Per Serving (4 Mini Pancakes): Calories 180, Total Fat 10g, Saturated Fat 3.5g, Cholesterol 50mg, Sodium 420mg, Total Carbohydrate 19g, Dietary Fiber 4g, Protein 5g*

note: These make a nice side dish to roasted pork or chicken.

mexican *rice*

preparation: 10 minutes • **processing:** 20–30 seconds • **cook time:** 30–40 minutes
yield: 4 cups (960 ml) (8 servings)

1 3/4 cups (420 ml) chicken broth

10 1/2 ounces (300 g) ripe tomatoes, quartered

2 garlic cloves, peeled, divided use

1 ounce (28 g) wedge yellow onion, peeled

2 Tablespoons (30 ml) canola oil

1/8 teaspoon salt

ground black pepper to taste

1 cup (185 g) uncooked white rice

chopped tomatoes, green chilies or sliced pimentos for garnish

1. Place broth, tomatoes, one garlic clove and onion into the Vitamix container and secure lid.

2. Select Variable 7.

3. Switch machine to Start and slowly increase speed to Variable 7.

4. Blend for 20 to 30 seconds. Set aside.

5. Heat oil in a 4-quart saucepan over medium heat. Chop remaining garlic clove and add to the oil. Add rice and cook until rice is golden brown, stirring frequently, about 6 minutes.

6. Stir in tomato mixture, season with 1/8 teaspoon salt and black pepper, and reduce heat to low. Cook, covered until rice is tender and has absorbed all the liquid, 30 to 40 minutes. Remove from heat and let sit covered for 10 minutes.

7. Garnish with chopped tomatoes, green chilies or sliced pimentos.

nutritional information: *Amount Per Serving: Calories 120, Total Fat 3.5g, Saturated Fat 0g, Cholesterol 0mg, Sodium 250mg, Total Carbohydrate 20g, Dietary Fiber 1g, Protein 2g*

fresh *slaw* with fennel seed *dressing*

preparation: 25 minutes • **processing:** 30 – 45 seconds plus Pulsing
chill time: 4 hours – overnight • **yield:** 10 1/4 cups (2.4 kg) (10 servings)

1 1/2 pound (680 g) head green cabbage, cored, cut into 1 1/2–inch (4 cm) chunks, divided use

9 ounce (256 g) fennel bulb, quartered

1 large red bell pepper,
9 ounces (256 g), quartered

4 1/2 ounces (128 g) carrot, cut into thirds

1 large Granny Smith apple, 7 1/2 ounces (213 g), small dice

2/3 cup (160 ml) white wine vinegar

1/4 cup (50 g) granulated sugar

2 1/4 teaspoons fennel seeds

1/2 cup (120 g) light mayonnaise

1/4 cup (60 g) reduced fat sour cream

1/3 cup (80 ml) extra virgin olive oil

1. Place half of the cabbage into the Vitamix container, fill with water to the 6 cup (1.4 l) level and secure lid.

2. Select Variable 6.

3. Pulse 5 times. Drain and place in large-size mixing bowl. Repeat with remaining cabbage.

4. Place fennel into the Vitamix container, fill with water to the 6 cup (1.4 l) level and secure lid.

5. Select Variable 6.

6. Pulse 5 times. Drain and remove to bowl containing cabbage.

7. Place red pepper quarters into the Vitamix container and secure lid.

8. Select Variable 4.

9. Pulse 5 to 6 times. Remove to bowl with other vegetables.

10. Repeat process with carrot chunks and remove to bowl. Add chopped apple to the vegetable mixture.

11. Place vinegar, sugar and fennel seeds into the Vitamix container and secure lid.

12. Select Variable 1.

13. Switch machine to Start and slowly increase speed to Variable 10.

14. Blend for 30 to 45 seconds. Stop machine; add mayo, sour cream and oil to the container and secure lid.

15. Select Variable 5.

16. Pulse 5 times until blended. Pour over chopped vegetables and toss to mix.

17. Cover and refrigerate at least 4 hours or overnight before serving.

>> **nutritional information:** *Amount Per Serving: Calories 190, Total Fat 12g, Saturated Fat 2g, Cholesterol 5mg, Sodium 120mg, Total Carbohydrate 18g, Dietary Fiber 4g, Protein 2g*

hawaiian style *coleslaw*

preparation: 20 minutes • **processing:** 10 seconds plus Pulsing
yield: 9 3/4 cups (2.3 kg) (19 servings)

2 pounds (908 g) cabbage, cut into 1 1/2–inch (4 cm) wedges

1 cup (165 g) fresh pineapple, cut into bite sized pieces

1 cup (189 g) canned mandarin oranges segments, drained

3/4 cup (101 g) blue cheese crumbles

1 1/2 cups (360 g) light mayonnaise

1/2 cup (100 g) chopped scallions

2 1/2 Tablespoons (38 ml) fresh lemon juice

1/4 teaspoon ground black pepper

1. Place half of the cabbage wedges into the Vitamix container, fill with water to the 6 cup (1.4 l) mark and secure lid.

2. Select Variable 6.

3. Pulse 5 to 6 times until chopped. Drain, remove to a large-size mixing bowl, and repeat with remaining cabbage.

4. Add pineapple, mandarin orange segments and blue cheese to the bowl containing the cabbage.

5. Place the mayonnaise, scallions, lemon juice and black pepper into the Vitamix container and secure lid.

6. Select Variable 1.

7. Switch machine to Start and slowly increase speed to Variable 2.

8. Blend for 10 seconds.

9. Pour over vegetables and toss to combine. Season to taste with kosher salt and pepper if necessary.

 nutritional information: *Amount Per 1/2 Cup (120 g) Serving: Calories 110, Total Fat 8g, Saturated Fat 2g, Cholesterol 15mg, Sodium 220mg, Total Carbohydrate 7g, Dietary Fiber 2g, Protein 2g*

hawaiian luau

Turn your next backyard barbeque into an island getaway. This coleslaw recipe makes almost 20 servings in a single blend, so it's an easy recipe when entertaining a large crowd. Make it ahead the day before to save even more time. Serve alongside grilled chicken kabobs with green, red, and yellow bell peppers, fresh pineapple chunks, and onion. Piña Colada Cocktails and Tropical Shakes (Beverages) complete the meal.

mains

beef

189 brown sugar citrus beef satay

fish

198 coconut fish curry

pork

177 chipotle bbq ribs with slaw

178 pork tenderloin in orange-ginger sauce

183 shallot oyster pork satay

185 thai pork satay

poultry

174 jerk chicken with pineapple mango salsa

176 sweet turkey burgers with mixed veggies

180 ground turkey sloppy joes

182 coconut curry chicken

184 brazilian chicken salad

192 curried tropical stir-fry

194 chop chop pocket sandwiches

vegetarian

179 zucchini burgers

186 macaroni with cheese sauce

188 indian vegetable stew

190 thin crust pineapple pizza

196 butternut squash ravioli with oregano hazelnut pesto

mains

beef • fish • pork • poultry • vegetarian

jerk chicken with
pineapple mango *salsa*

preparation: 20 minutes • **processing:** 40 seconds plus Pulsing • **cook time:** 10 minutes
yield: 1 1/2 cups (360 ml) jerk seasoning; 2 1/2 cups (600 g) salsa (4 servings)

2 cups (375 g) frozen unsweetened
pineapple, thawed or 2 cups (330 g)
fresh pineapple

1 medium onion, 3 ounces (85 g)
rough chopped

2 teaspoons dried thyme

2 teaspoons garlic salt

1/2 teaspoon ground allspice

1/2 teaspoon ground cinnamon

1/2 teaspoon ground black pepper

1/4 teaspoon cayenne pepper

4 6-ounce (170 g) boneless skinless
chicken breasts

1. Place pineapple, onion, thyme, garlic salt, allspice, cinnamon, black pepper and cayenne pepper into the Vitamix container and secure lid.

2. Select Variable 1.

3. Switch machine to Start and slowly increase speed to Variable 5.

4. Blend for 30 seconds. Stop, scrape down sides, and replace lid. Blend an additional 10 seconds.

5. Rub mixture onto chicken breasts. Grill chicken, turning halfway through cooking until center reaches an internal temperature of 170°F (77°C).

6. Serve chicken breasts along side or topped with Pineapple Mango Salsa.

pineapple mango salsa:

2 cups (330 g) fresh pineapple chunks

2 cups (330 g) fresh mango chunks

1/4 cup (5 g) packed fresh cilantro leaves

1 1/2 teaspoons lime zest

1/8 large jalapeño

salt to taste

1. Place all Salsa ingredients into the Vitamix container and secure lid.

2. Select Variable 6.

3. Pulse 10 times until all ingredients are chopped. If large pieces still remain, reduce speed to Variable 3 and Pulse a few more times.

>> **nutritional information:** *Amount Per Serving: Calories 370, Total Fat 5g, Saturated Fat 1g, Cholesterol 110mg, Sodium 640mg, Total Carbohydrate 46g, Dietary Fiber 3g, Protein 38g*

sweet turkey *burgers* with *mixed veggies*

preparation: 10 minutes • **processing:** Pulsing • **cook time:** 15 minutes • **yield:** 4 burgers

1 medium carrot, 2 1/2 ounce (71 g) cut into 3 pieces

2 green onions, cut into 2-inch (5 cm) pieces

3 Tablespoons (21 g) dry bread crumbs

1/4 teaspoon Italian seasoning

1/8 teaspoon salt

1/8 teaspoon ground black pepper

12 ounces (341 g) ground turkey breast

4 whole wheat hamburger buns, split and toasted

1/2 cup (139 g) whole cranberry sauce

1 cup (30 g) mixed baby greens

1. Place carrot pieces into the Vitamix container and secure lid.

2. Select Variable 5.

3. Pulse 10 times to chop finely. Do not remove.

4. Return the Vitamix container to its base and secure lid. Select Variable 2 and remove the lid plug.

5. Switch machine to Start and drop onion pieces through the lid plug opening. Stop machine and remove lid.

6. To the carrot and onion mixture, add bread crumbs, spices, turkey breast and secure lid.

7. Select Variable 4.

8. Pulse 10 times until mixture is fully combined. Form into 4 large patties.

9. Grill patties uncovered over medium heat, 350°F (180°C), for 12 to 15 minutes or until patties are done, turning once halfway through.

10. Serve on hamburger buns topped with cranberry sauce and baby greens.

>> **nutritional information:** *Amount Per Burger: Calories 290, Total Fat 2.5g, Saturated Fat 0g, Cholesterol 35mg, Sodium 400mg, Total Carbohydrate 41g, Dietary Fiber 5g, Protein 26g*

chipotle bbq *ribs* with *slaw*

preparation: 20 minutes • **processing:** 20 seconds • **cook time:** 3–3 1/2 hours • **yield:** 7 servings

3 1/2 pounds (1.6 kg) pork loin back ribs or meaty pork spareribs

1 cup (245 g) no-salt added tomato sauce

1 cup (240 ml) barbecue sauce

2 canned chipotle chilies in adobo sauce

2 Tablespoons (16 g) cornstarch

2 Tablespoons (30 ml) water

1. Preheat broiler. Cut ribs into two rib portions. Place ribs on the unheated rack of a broiler pan. Broil 6-inches (15 cm) from the heat, about 10 minutes or until brown, turning once. Transfer ribs to a 4 to 5 quart slow cooker.

2. Place tomato sauce, barbecue sauce, and chipotle chilies into the Vitamix container and secure lid.

3. Select Variable 1.

4. Switch machine to Start and slowly increase speed to Variable 3.

5. Blend for 20 seconds. Pour over ribs in the slow cooker.

6. Cover and cook on High for 3 to 3 1/2 hours. Transfer ribs to a serving platter, reserving cooking liquid. Cover ribs to keep warm. Skim fat from cooking liquid.

7. Turn slow cooker to High heat setting. Combine cornstarch and water in a small bowl. Stir into liquid in the slow cooker. Cover and cook 15 minutes, or until thickened. Serve ribs with sauce.

 nutritional information: *Amount Per Serving (2 Ribs): Calories 580, Total Fat 37g, Saturated Fat 13g, Cholesterol 160mg, Sodium 500mg, Total Carbohydrate 17g, Dietary Fiber 1g, Protein 44g*

note: Broiling makes the ribs less fatty but this step may be omitted if desired. Serve ribs with coleslaw, which adds a cooling crunch to the spicy BBQ sauce.

pork tenderloin in orange-ginger *sauce*

preparation: 15 minutes • **processing:** 15–20 seconds • **cook time:** 13–15 minutes
yield: 5 servings

1 1/4–1 1/2 pounds (568–680 g)
pork tenderloin

1/2 teaspoon salt

1/4 teaspoon ground black pepper

1 orange, peeled, halved, plus 1-inch x
2-inch (2.5 cm x 5 cm) strip orange zest

2 thin slices fresh ginger

1 teaspoon dark sesame oil

1 cup (240 ml) chicken broth

2 Tablespoons (30 ml) honey

1 Tablespoon cornstarch

1 Tablespoon vegetable oil

1 small red bell pepper cut in
thin bite-size strips

2 Tablespoons (12 g) sliced green onions

1. Cut tenderloin crosswise into 5 pieces. Place each piece cut side down between pieces of plastic wrap. Pound to 1/4-inch (.6 cm) thickness with meat mallet or rolling pin, starting at center. Season with salt and pepper. Set aside.

2. Place orange, ginger, sesame oil, broth, honey and cornstarch into the Vitamix container and secure lid.

3. Select Variable 1.

4. Switch machine to Start and slowly increase speed to Variable 7. Blend for 15 to 20 seconds.

5. Heat oil in 12-inch (30 cm) nonstick skillet over medium-high heat. Add pork. Cook 8 to 10 minutes or until deep golden brown, turning once. Remove from skillet; add bell pepper. Cook 2 minutes. Add pork back to skillet. Pour orange mixture into skillet. Cook 3 minutes or until bubbly and thickened, and pork is no longer pink, stirring occasionally. Serve sauce over pork. Sprinkle with green onions.

 nutritional information: *Amount Per Serving: Calories 220, Total Fat 7g, Saturated Fat 1.5g, Cholesterol 80mg, Sodium 496mg, Total Carbohydrate 13g, Dietary Fiber 1g, Protein 26g*

zucchini *burgers*

preparation: 15 minutes • **processing:** Pulsing • **cook time:** 6 minutes • **yield:** 17 patties

2 pounds (908 g) zucchini, cut into large chunks

1 large onion, peeled, quartered, about 1 1/4 cups (195 g) chopped

1 1/2 cups (180 g) Italian seasoned dry breadcrumbs

3 large eggs

1/2 cup (50 g) shredded Romano or Parmesan cheese

1/2 teaspoon garlic powder

1/2 teaspoon onion powder

1/2 teaspoon dried parsley

1/2 teaspoon dried basil

1/2 teaspoon dried oregano

Canola oil for frying

1. Place zucchini into the Vitamix container, float with water and secure lid.

2. Select Variable 6.

3. Pulse 5 times until chopped. Strain in a colander. Place towel or paper towel over top to pat dry.

4. Place onion into the Vitamix container and secure lid.

5. Select Variable 4.

6. Pulse 4 to 5 times to evenly chop. Combine zucchini, onion, breadcrumbs, eggs, cheese and spices in a large bowl and stir until evenly combined.

7. Heat a large 12–inch (30 cm) heavy-bottomed skillet over medium high heat. Pour 1/4 cup (60 ml) oil in pan. When oil is hot, measure 1/4 cup (60 g) portions of the zucchini mixture into pan.

8. Spread gently to form a patty. Cook 3 minutes or until the underside is crispy and dark brown.

9. Flip and cook an additional 3 minutes. Remove to a paper towel-lined plate.

nutritional information: *Amount Per Patty: Calories 80, Total Fat 2.5g, Saturated Fat 1g, Cholesterol 35mg, Sodium 240mg, Total Carbohydrate 10g, Dietary Fiber 1g, Protein 5g*

ground turkey *sloppy joes*

preparation: 30 minutes • **processing:** 30 seconds • **cook time:** 25 minutes • **yield:** 8 servings

1/4 cup (30 g) shelled pistachios

2 Tablespoons (30 ml) vegetable oil

1 Tablespoon chopped fresh ginger root

2 garlic cloves, peeled, halved

1/2 jalapeño pepper, chopped

1 teaspoon garam masala

1/2 teaspoon paprika

15-ounce (425 g) can tomato sauce

2 Tablespoons (30 ml) water

4 Tablespoons (60 ml) vegetable oil, divided use

1/4 cup (36 g) raisins

1 teaspoon cumin seeds

1 medium onion, 5 ounces (142 g) diced

1 medium red bell pepper, 8 ounces (227 g) seeded, diced

1/8 teaspoon cayenne pepper

kosher salt

1 pound (454 g) ground turkey

1/2 teaspoon honey

1/4 cup (60 ml) half & half

1/4 cup (4 g) chopped cilantro leaves

8 sesame buns

1. Place pistachios into the Vitamix container and secure lid.

2. Select Variable 4.

3. Pulse 3 times to chop. Set aside.

4. Heat vegetable oil in a small saucepan over medium heat. Add ginger, garlic and jalapeño; cook for 1 minute. Remove from heat.

5. Place cooked mixture, garam masala, paprika, tomato sauce, and 2 Tablespoons (30 ml) water into the Vitamix container and secure lid.

6. Select Variable 4.

7. Switch machine to Start and slowly increase speed to Variable 10.

8. Blend for 30 seconds. Reserve.

9. To prepare the sloppy joes, heat 2 Tablespoons (30 ml) vegetable oil in a large skillet over medium heat. Add the raisins and chopped pistachios. Cook until the raisins swell, about 1 minute. Remove from skillet.

10. Add the remaining oil to the skillet and add cumin seeds, onion, and bell pepper. Cook until softened, about 5 minutes. Add cayenne pepper, salt to taste and turkey, cooking until opaque, about 5 minutes. Break up turkey as you cook to form small crumbles.

11. Add reserved sauce to the skillet. Stir and bring to a boil, then reduce heat to low and simmer until mixture thickens slightly, about 10 minutes.

12. Stir in honey, half & half, raisins, and pistachios. Stir in chopped cilantro before serving. Serve on toasted sesame seed buns.

nutritional information: *Amount Per Serving: Calories 440, Total Fat 22g, Saturated Fat 4.5g, Cholesterol 45mg, Sodium 690mg, Total Carbohydrate 43g, Dietary Fiber 3g, Protein 19g*

coconut curry *chicken*

preparation: 20 minutes • ***processing:*** 3 minutes • ***cook time:*** 10 minutes
bake time: 1 1/2 hours • ***yield:*** 4 servings; 3 cups (720 ml) sauce

1/4 cup (65 g) peanut butter

14–ounce (400 ml) can unsweetened light coconut milk

1/3 cup (80 ml) reduced sodium chicken broth

2 Tablespoons (30 ml) reduced sodium soy sauce

2 Tablespoons (30 ml) rice vinegar

1 Tablespoon packed brown sugar

1 Tablespoon toasted sesame oil

2 teaspoons red curry paste

1 teaspoon fresh ginger root

1 garlic clove, peeled

1/8–1/4 teaspoon cayenne pepper

1/2 cup (63 g) all-purpose flour

1/2 teaspoon salt

1/2 teaspoon ground black pepper

3 pounds (1.4 kg) chicken bone-in parts (legs, thighs, breasts)

2 Tablespoons (30 ml) vegetable oil

2 Tablespoons (2 g) chopped fresh cilantro leaves

2 cups (316 g) cooked rice

1. Place peanut butter, coconut milk, broth, soy sauce, vinegar, brown sugar, sesame oil, red curry paste, ginger, garlic, and cayenne pepper into the Vitamix container and secure lid.

2. Select Variable 1.

3. Switch machine to Start and slowly increase speed to Variable 5.

4. Blend for 10 seconds. Stop and scrape sides. Switch machine to Start and blend an additional 3 minutes. Set aside.

5. Preheat oven to 300°F (150°C).

6. In a plastic bag, combine flour, salt, and black pepper. Add chicken pieces to flour mixture, shaking to coat.

7. In a large skillet, cook chicken in hot oil until brown. Transfer to an ungreased rectangular baking dish, pour sauce over chicken, cover with foil, and bake for 1 hour. Bake uncovered for 20 to 30 minutes more until chicken is very tender.

8. Transfer to a serving platter. Spoon sauce over chicken, sprinkle with cilantro, and serve over cooked rice.

 nutritional information: *Amount Per Serving (with 1/4 Cup (60 g) Sauce): Calories 690, Total Fat 23g, Saturated Fat 6g, Cholesterol 225mg, Sodium 870mg, Total Carbohydrate 38g, Dietary Fiber 1g, Protein 80g*

shallot oyster pork *satay*

preparation: 15 minutes • **processing:** 30 seconds
cook time: 5 minutes • **chill time:** 2–4 hours
yield: 2 cups (480 ml) sauce (7 servings)

6 Tablespoons (90 ml) canola oil

1/4 cup (60 ml) oyster sauce

1/4 cup (19 g) chopped lemongrass

1/4 cup (32 g) toasted sesame seeds

2 Tablespoons (30 ml) fish sauce

2 teaspoons granulated sugar

3 ounces (85 g) shallots

2 garlic cloves, peeled

1 pound (454 g) pork strips, 1–inch x 1/4–inch (2.5 cm x .6 cm)

15 wooden skewers, soaked in water for 30 minutes

1. Place oil, oyster sauce, lemongrass, sesame seeds, fish sauce, sugar, shallots, and garlic into the Vitamix container and secure lid.

2. Select Variable 1.

3. Switch machine to Start and slowly increase speed to Variable 5.

4. Blend for 30 seconds.

5. Combine sauce with pork strips and chill for 2 to 4 hours.

6. Fold strip on to itself and insert skewer through the center, stretching the meat down the length of the skewer.

7. Grill until lightly charred, about 5 minutes.

bright idea

Soak skewers in water for 30 minutes prior to cooking to prevent them from burning. If unable to grill during the winter months, you can sauté instead. Heat 1 Tablespoon olive oil over medium-high heat. Add pork and sauté for 3 to 4 minutes per side or until cooked through.

nutritional information: *Amount Per Serving: Calories 260, Total Fat 22g, Saturated Fat 3.5g, Cholesterol 30mg, Sodium 720mg, Total Carbohydrate 6g, Dietary Fiber 1g, Protein 9g*

brazilian chicken *salad*

preparation: 20 minutes • **processing:** 20 seconds plus Pulsing
yield: 5 3/4 cups (1.4 kg) (11 servings)

2 pounds (908 g) skinless boneless chicken breast, cooked, cut into 2–inch (5 cm) pieces, cooled

11–ounce (312 g) can mandarin oranges, drained

1/2 of 15 1/4–ounce (432 g) can tropical mixed fruit, drained

1/2 cup (54 g) toasted slivered almonds

1 1/2 cups (360 g) low-fat mayonnaise

2 Tablespoons (12 g) lemon zest

2 Tablespoons (30 ml) fresh lemon juice

1 teaspoon garlic salt

1 teaspoon ground ginger

1/2 teaspoon cayenne pepper

1. Place chicken into the Vitamix container and secure lid.

2. Select Variable 6.

3. Pulse 3 to 5 times. Remove to a large-size mixing bowl. Mix in mandarin oranges, tropical mixed fruit and slivered almonds.

4. Place mayonnaise, lemon zest, lemon juice, garlic salt, ground ginger and cayenne pepper into the Vitamix container and secure lid.

5. Select Variable 2.

6. Switch machine to Start and blend for 10 seconds. Stop, scrape and blend an additional 10 seconds.

7. Add to the fruit and chicken mixture. Mix by hand until combined.

8. Serve 1/2 cup (188 g) on baby spinach greens or use as a sandwich filling.

>> **nutritional information:** *Amount Per Serving: Calories 260, Total Fat 15g, Saturated Fat 2g, Cholesterol 60mg, Sodium 370mg, Total Carbohydrate 13g, Dietary Fiber 1g, Protein 18g*

thai pork *satay*

---

preparation: 20 minutes • **processing:** 30 seconds • **cook time:** 10 minutes • **chill time:** 4 hours
yield: 20 skewers (10 servings)

2 cups (480 ml) light coconut milk, divided use

1 ounce (28 g) lemon grass

1/4 cup (60 ml) coconut oil

2 Tablespoons (18 g) chopped fresh ginger root

2 Tablespoons (28 g) dark brown sugar

1 Tablespoon ground turmeric

1 Tablespoon ground coriander

2 teaspoons kosher salt

1 teaspoon ground cumin

1/4 teaspoon cayenne pepper

1 1/2 pounds (680 g) pork loin, cut into 1-inch x 1/4-inch (2.5 cm x .6 cm) slices

20 wooden skewers, soaked in water for 30 minutes

1. Place 1 cup (240 ml) coconut milk, lemon grass, oil, ginger, sugar, turmeric, coriander, salt, cumin and cayenne pepper into the Vitamix container and secure lid.

2. Select Variable 1.

3. Switch machine to Start and slowly increase speed to Variable 7.

4. Blend for 20 seconds. Stop; scrape down sides of container and blend an additional 15 seconds.

5. Toss pork with sauce in a bowl; chill 4 hours.

6. Pour remaining 1 cup (240 ml) coconut milk into a bowl and stir to combine. Thread 3 slices of pork onto each skewer, dip into coconut milk, and grill until lightly charred, about 7 minutes.

» **nutritional information:** *Amount Per Serving: Calories 200, Total Fat 14g, Saturated Fat 10g, Cholesterol 35mg, Sodium 640mg, Total Carbohydrate 6g, Dietary Fiber 0g, Protein 13g*

macaroni with cheese *sauce*

preparation: 15 minutes • **processing:** 4–5 minutes • **bake time:** 30 minutes
yield: 6 servings

2 cups (210 g) elbow macaroni, uncooked

1/4 cup (60 g) butter

1/4 cup (30 g) all-purpose flour

1/4 teaspoon salt

1 1/3 cups (320 ml) milk

1/2 teaspoon yellow mustard

1 1/2 cups (173 g) cubed American cheese or other mild yellow cheese

crumb topping:

2 slices bread, white or wheat

1 teaspoon butter

dash garlic powder

dash black pepper

dash dried oregano

dash onion powder

dash cayenne pepper

1. Preheat oven to 350°F (180°C).

2. Cook macaroni as directed on package. Drain.

3. Spray an 8-inch x 8-inch (20 cm x 20 cm) baking dish with vegetable cooking spray then add macaroni to dish.

4. Place butter, flour, salt, milk and mustard into the Vitamix container in the order listed and secure lid.

5. Select Variable 1.

6. Switch machine to Start and slowly increase speed to Variable 10.

7. Blend for 4 minutes or until steam escapes from the vented lid. As mixture thickens, it will not splash as much.

8. Reduce speed to Variable 1 and remove the lid plug. Add cheese through the lid plug opening.

9. Blend for 30 seconds.

10. Pour mixture over macaroni and mix thoroughly.

to make crumb topping:

1. Toast and butter 2 pieces of bread and cut into quarters.

2. Select Variable 2.

3. Switch machine to Start and remove the lid plug.

4. Drop bread through the lid plug opening. Blend until you have crumbs. Add seasonings to the crumbs.

5. Cover with crumb topping mixture and bake until top is golden brown, about 30 minutes.

nutritional information: Amount Per Serving: Calories 380, Total Fat 20g, Saturated Fat 12g, Cholesterol 55mg, Sodium 650mg, Total Carbohydrate 38g, Dietary Fiber 1g, Protein 13g

indian vegetable *stew*

preparation: 20 minutes • **processing:** 10–15 seconds • **cook time:** 40 minutes
yield: 4 servings

1-inch (2.5 cm) piece fresh ginger root

2 garlic cloves, peeled

15-ounce (425 g) can diced tomatoes

1/2 teaspoon cayenne pepper

2 Tablespoons (30 ml) canola oil

4 ounces (114 g) onion, chopped (1 medium)

1/2 large yellow bell pepper,
4 1/2 ounces diced

8 ounces (227 g) boiling potatoes,
peeled, cubed

2 medium carrots, 5 ounces (142 g) sliced

1 1/2 teaspoons garam masala

1/2 teaspoon chili powder

3 cups (300 g) cauliflower florets
(3/4 pound)

1/2 cup (120 ml) light coconut milk

ground black pepper to taste

1. Place ginger, garlic, tomatoes and cayenne into the Vitamix container and secure lid.

2. Select Variable 1.

3. Switch machine to Start and slowly increase speed to Variable 5.

4. Blend for 10 to 15 seconds. Set aside.

5. Heat oil in a saucepan over medium heat. Add onion and bell pepper, and sauté 10 minutes, or until softened. Stir in potatoes, carrots, garam masala and chili powder. Cover and cook over medium-low heat for 10 minutes, stirring occasionally.

6. Add cauliflower, tomato mixture and 1/2 cup (120 ml) water. Simmer 20 minutes covered. Remove from heat and stir in coconut milk. Season with black pepper.

>> **nutritional information:** *Amount Per Serving: Calories 210, Total Fat 10g, Saturated Fat 2.5g, Cholesterol 0mg, Sodium 300mg, Total Carbohydrate 29g, Dietary Fiber 5g, Protein 5g*

brown sugar citrus beef *satay*

preparation: 15 minutes • **processing:** 40 seconds • **cook time:** 5 minutes
yield: 24 skewers (12 servings)

1/2 cup (120 ml) low sodium soy sauce

1/2 cup (8 g) packed fresh cilantro leaves

4 Tablespoons (24 g) orange zest

2 Tablespoons (30 ml) plus 2 teaspoons fish sauce

1 Tablespoon dark brown sugar

2 teaspoons canola oil

5 garlic cloves, peeled

2 pounds (908 g) beef sirloin, cut into 1–inch x 1/4–inch (2.5 cm x .6 cm) slices

24 wooden skewers, soaked in water for 30 minutes

1. Place soy sauce, cilantro, orange zest, fish sauce, sugar, oil and garlic into the Vitamix container and secure lid.

2. Select Variable 1.

3. Switch machine to Start and slowly increase speed to Variable 5.

4. Blend for 30 seconds. Stop, scrape down sides and secure lid.

5. Select Variable 1.

6. Switch machine to Start and slowly increase speed to Variable 2. Blend for an additional 10 seconds.

7. Toss beef with sauce in bowl. Chill 4 hours.

8. Fold strip on to itself and insert skewer through the center, stretching the meat down the length of the skewer.

9. Grill until lightly charred, about 5 minutes.

 **nutritional information:** *Amount Per Serving: Calories 120, Total Fat 3.5g, Saturated Fat 1g, Cholesterol 45mg, Sodium 750mg, Total Carbohydrate 3g, Dietary Fiber 0g, Protein 18g*

note: Marinade will impart a green tint to the beef due to the cilantro.

thin crust pineapple *pizza*

preparation: 25 minutes • ***processing:*** 1 1/2 minutes • ***bake time:*** 35 minutes
yield: 8 slices (1 large pizza)

1 1/2 cups (248 g) diced fresh pineapple

1 teaspoon brown sugar

12 ounces (340 g) onion, sliced

1 teaspoon fresh rosemary

1 teaspoon fresh thyme

2 Tablespoons (30 ml) olive oil

3 1/2 ounces (100 g) Romano and Asiago cheese chunks

1/4 cup (60 g) mayonnaise

1 Tablespoon chopped fresh basil

2 small garlic cloves, peeled, chopped

thin crust pizza dough (see recipe below)

1/4 cup (28 g) sun-dried tomatoes, thin sliced

1 1/2 teaspoons crushed red pepper flakes

1 Tablespoon chopped fresh basil

1. Preheat oven to 400°F (200°C). Combine pineapple and brown sugar in a baking pan and roast for 10 minutes. Toss sliced onions with herbs and olive oil. Roast on a separate baking sheet 10 minutes or until slightly browned. Set aside.

2. Place Romano and Asiago cheese chunks into the Vitamix container and secure lid.

3. Select Variable 1.

4. Switch machine to Start and slowly increase speed to Variable 3.

5. Pulse 20 times. Measure out 1 1/4 cups (125 g) grated cheese. Set aside.

6. Combine mayonnaise, basil, and garlic by hand in a small bowl. Set aside.

7. Prepare pizza dough.

thin crust pizza dough:

3 lightly filled and leveled cups (375 g) all-purpose flour

1 3/4 teaspoons instant fast rise yeast

1 1/4 teaspoons salt

8–11 ounces (240–320 ml) hot water

3 3/4 teaspoons olive oil

1. Preheat oven to 425°F (220°C).

2. Place flour, yeast, and salt into the Vitamix container and secure lid.

3. Select Variable 1.

4. Switch machine to Start and slowly increase speed to Variable 8. Blend for 5 seconds. Turn machine off and remove the lid plug.

5. Select Variable 3.

6. Pulse about 60 short times in 45 seconds while slowly adding oil and water through the lid plug opening until a ball forms.

7. After ball has formed Pulse continuously for 10 to 15 seconds.

8. With floured hands, remove dough and form into a round ball. Place in a greased bowl, turning over to grease all around. Let rise 10 minutes for a thin crust. Stretch into pizza and top as desired. Bake for 12 to 15 minutes.

make-your-own-pizza night

Instead of ordering in next Friday night, turn your kitchen into a pizza parlor. Set up prep stations where everyone can roll out pizza dough and assemble their own made-to-order pies.

For planning ahead, prepare two batches of dough. Shape unused dough and place on a cookie sheet in the freezer until firm, remove, wrap well, and freeze up to 1 month. Then, thaw in the fridge the night before use. Dough can be used for another pizza night or rolled into bread sticks and served with pasta.

nutritional information: *Amount Per Slice: Calories 370, Total Fat 16g, Saturated Fat 4g, Cholesterol 15mg, Sodium 600mg, Total Carbohydrate 46g, Dietary Fiber 3g, Protein 10g*

curried tropical *stir-fry*

preparation: 20 minutes • **processing:** 8 minutes • **cook time:** 40 minutes plus marinade time
yield: 6 servings

2 Tablespoons (30 ml) soy sauce

1 Tablespoon curry powder

2 Tablespoons (30 ml) vegetable oil

2 Tablespoons (30 ml) sesame oil

6 5-ounce (142 g) boneless skinless chicken breast halves, sliced 1/4-inch (.6 cm) thick

1 cup (240 ml) pineapple juice

2/3 cup (160 ml) apricot nectar

1 Tablespoon white vinegar

1/4 cup (40 g) potato starch mixed with 1/3 cup (80 ml) apricot nectar

6 ounces (170 g) red bell pepper, cut 1/2-inch (1.3 cm) dice

2 Tablespoons (30 ml) vegetable oil

1 cup (240 g) tropical fruit salad, drained

4 cups (632 g) cooked white rice

1/3 cup (30 g) sliced toasted almonds

1/3 cup (33 g) sliced green onions

1. Place soy sauce, curry, vegetable oil, and sesame oil into the Vitamix container and secure lid.

2. Select Variable 1.

3. Switch machine to Start and slowly increase speed to Variable 3.

4. Blend for 10 seconds.

5. Place chicken in a bowl and pour marinade over. Refrigerate for 1 to 4 hours.

6. Place pineapple juice, apricot nectar, and vinegar into the Vitamix container and secure lid.

7. Select Variable 1.

8. Switch machine to Start and slowly increase speed to Variable 10.

9. Blend for 5 minutes.

10. Reduce speed to Variable 1, remove lid plug, and pour apricot potato starch mixture through the lid plug opening. Replace lid plug and slowly increase speed to Variable 10. Blend for 1 minute. Set aside.

11. Sauté peppers in 2 Tablespoons (30 ml) vegetable oil for 10 minutes until tender. Remove to a plate. Add chicken in batches, cooking until chicken is no longer pink and juices run clear.

12. Mix cooked chicken with bell peppers, tropical fruit salad, and apricot sauce. Serve over cooked rice, and top with a sprinkle of toasted almonds and green onions.

>> ***nutritional information:*** *Amount Per Serving: Calories 550, Total Fat 21g, Saturated Fat 3g, Cholesterol 90mg, Sodium 510mg, Total Carbohydrate 55g, Dietary Fiber 2g, Protein 35g*

chop chop pocket *sandwiches*

preparation: 15 minutes • ***processing:*** Pulsing • ***yield:*** 8 sandwiches

1 cup (100 g) walnut halves

1 carrot, 4 ounces (114 g), quartered

6 large radishes

6-inch (15 cm) zucchini, cut in 1 1/2-inch (4 cm) sections

2 4 1/2-ounce (128 g) cooked boneless skinless chicken breasts, each cut in 3 pieces

2 cups (140 g) chopped iceberg lettuce

1 cup (240 g) blue cheese dressing

1/2 teaspoon kosher salt

1/4 teaspoon ground black pepper

8 whole wheat pita pocket halves

1. Place walnuts into the Vitamix container and secure lid.

2. Select Variable 6. Pulse 3 times. Pour into large bowl.

3. Place carrots into the Vitamix container and secure lid.

4. Select Variable 7. Pulse 3 times. Place in bowl with nuts.

5. Place radishes and zucchini into the Vitamix container and secure lid.

6. Select Variable 6. Pulse 4 times. Add to bowl.

7. Place chicken into the Vitamix container and secure lid.

8. Select Variable 6. Pulse 3 times. Add to bowl.

9. Add lettuce and dressing to bowl. Add salt and pepper. Toss to mix well. Spoon into pita halves.

>> **nutritional information:** *Amount Per Sandwich: Calories 370, Total Fat 26g, Saturated Fat 3.5g, Cholesterol 35mg, Sodium 620mg, Total Carbohydrate 22g, Dietary Fiber 4g, Protein 16g*

butternut squash *ravioli* with oregano hazelnut *pesto*

preparation: 25 minutes • **processing:** 1 minute 10 seconds • **cook time:** 10 minutes
bake time: 30 minutes • **yield:** 40 ravioli; 2 cups (480 g) pesto (8 servings)

pesto:

1 cup (240 ml) extra virgin olive oil

1 1/2 cups (72 g) packed fresh oregano leaves

1/2 cup (12 g) packed fresh basil leaves

1/2 cup (50 g) grated Parmesan cheese

1/4 cup (34 g) hazelnuts, toasted

2 garlic cloves, peeled

1. Place all Pesto ingredients into the Vitamix container in the order listed and secure lid.
2. Select Variable 1.
3. Switch machine to Start and slowly increase speed to Variable 6.
4. Blend for 30 seconds. Set aside.

ravioli:

2 Tablespoons (30 ml) olive oil

4 garlic cloves, peeled

1 small butternut squash, about 1 3/4 pounds (794 g), seeds removed or 2 cups (410 g) cooked winter squash, any variety

1 cup (100 g) grated Parmesan cheese

4 Tablespoons (57 g) unsalted butter, browned

1 Tablespoon grated nutmeg

2 teaspoons fresh sage

2 teaspoons fresh oregano

kosher salt and ground black pepper to taste

80 square wonton wrappers

1 egg, lightly beaten

ingredient IQ

Browned butter is made by cooking butter long enough to turn the milk solids and salt particles brown while cooking out any water present. It adds a rich, nutty, unmistakable flavor to this dish. Be careful not to burn the butter; stir continuously and maintain a low to medium heat while cooking.

Toast the hazelnuts over medium heat in a dry skillet. Toss or stir frequently to prevent burning. Toast until they are a light golden brown.

1. Heat oven to 450°F (230°C). Rub garlic and squash with 2 Tablespoons (30 ml) olive oil. Wrap garlic in foil and place directly on oven rack. Place squash, cut side down on baking sheet. Bake until tender, 30 minutes. Let cool 15 minutes before scooping out. If using cooked squash, only roast the garlic.

2. Place squash, garlic, Parmesan, butter, nutmeg, sage, oregano, salt and pepper into the Vitamix container and secure lid.

3. Select Variable 1.

4. Switch machine to Start and slowly increase speed to Variable 3.

5. Blend for 20 to 30 seconds using the tamper to press the ingredients into the blades. Stop machine, scrape sides and repeat.

6. Place 1 wonton wrapper on a work surface and fill with 1 Tablespoon of ravioli filling. Brush sides with egg and top with another wrapper. Seal edges. Repeat with remaining wrappers and filling.

7. Bring a large pot of salted water to a boil. Working in batches of 8–10, add ravioli, and cook until tender, about 2 minutes.

8. Portion onto plates and top with pesto.

nutritional information: *Amount Per Serving: Calories 720, Total Fat 47g, Saturated Fat 12g, Cholesterol 60mg, Sodium 740mg, Total Carbohydrate 56g, Dietary Fiber 4g, Protein 17g*

coconut fish *curry*

preparation: 30 minutes • **processing:** Pulsing • **cook time:** 15 minutes • **yield:** 4 servings

2 ounces (56 g) shallots, halved

9 1/2 ounce (270 g) red bell pepper, cut into 2-inch (5 cm) pieces

1/2-inch (1.3 cm) cube fresh ginger root

1 Tablespoon vegetable oil

2 1/2 teaspoons Thai red curry paste

14 ounce (414 ml) can light unsweetened coconut milk

1 Tablespoon fish sauce

zest of 2 limes

2 Tablespoons (30 ml) fresh lime juice

1 pound (454 g) halibut fillets, cut into 1 1/2-inch (4 cm) chunks

1/2 pound (227 g) peeled, deveined, uncooked shrimp

1/3 cup (5 g) chopped fresh cilantro leaves

1/3 cup (8 g) chopped fresh basil leaves

rice noodles or jasmine rice for serving

1. Place shallots, pepper, and ginger into the Vitamix container and secure lid.

2. Select Variable 5.

3. Pulse 3 times. Stop and scrape down sides of container. Pulse 2 more times.

4. Heat oil in a large saucepan over medium-high heat. Add chopped shallots, pepper, and ginger. Sauté until peppers are softened, about 5 minutes. Stir in curry paste, coconut milk, fish sauce, lime zest, and lime juice. Simmer gently, stirring often, about 5 minutes.

5. Add fish and shrimp to sauce. Return to a simmer and cook until fish and shrimp are opaque in the center, about 5 to 6 minutes. Season to taste with salt and pepper. Stir in cilantro and basil.

6. Serve over rice noodles or jasmine rice.

>> **nutritional information:** *Amount Per Serving: Calories 280, Total Fat 13g, Saturated Fat 7g, Cholesterol 125mg, Sodium 850mg, Total Carbohydrate 10g, Dietary Fiber 2g, Protein 30g*

sauces & spreads

pestos

sauces

spreads

sauces & spreads

pestos • sauces • spreads

homemade *peanut butter*

preparation: 5 minutes • ***processing:*** 1 minute 30 seconds • ***yield:*** 2 cups (480 ml) (16 servings)

4 cups (590 g) unsalted dry roasted peanuts

1. Place nuts into the Vitamix container and secure lid.

2. Select Variable 1.

3. Switch machine to Start and slowly increase speed to Variable 10.

4. Use the tamper to press the ingredients into the blades.

5. In 1 minute you will hear a high-pitched chugging sound.

6. Blend for an additional 30 seconds or until desired consistency is reached.

7. Store in an airtight container in the refrigerator for up to 1 week. It can also be frozen for longer storage.

 nutritional information: *Amount Per 2 Tablespoon (30 g) Serving: Calories 210, Total Fat 18g, Saturated Fat 2.5g, Cholesterol 0mg, Sodium 0mg, Total Carbohydrate 8g, Dietary Fiber 3g, Protein 9g*

balsamic herbed *butter*

preparation: 20 minutes • **processing:** 20–30 seconds • **cook time:** 35 minutes
yield: 2 1/4 cups (540 ml) (36 servings)

4 cups (480 ml) balsamic vinegar

4 teaspoons whole black peppercorns

4 teaspoons honey

4 Tablespoons (8 g) fresh rosemary

1 1/2 cups (340 g) unsalted butter, slightly softened

1 teaspoon kosher salt

1. Combine the vinegar and peppercorns in a small saucepan over high heat and cook, stirring occasionally until reduced to about 1/2 cup (120 ml), about 35 to 40 minutes.

2. Strain peppercorns and measure out 1/2 cup (120 ml). Whisk in honey and rosemary. Let cool to room temperature.

3. Place cooled mixture, butter and salt into the Vitamix container and secure lid.

4. Select Variable 3.

5. Switch machine to Start and blend for 20 to 30 seconds. Stop and scrape sides with a spatula and blend an additional 5 to 10 seconds.

6. Serve with meats like grilled steak, or serve alongside regular butter with bread.

 nutritional information: *Amount Per 1 Tablespoon Serving: Calories 100, Total Fat 8g, Saturated Fat 5g, Cholesterol 20mg, Sodium 60mg, Total Carbohydrate 6g, Dietary Fiber 0g, Protein 0g*

trapanese pesto *sauce*

preparation: 15 minutes • ***processing:*** 40 seconds plus Pulsing • ***cook time:*** 5 – 7 minutes
yield: 3 cups (720 ml) (24 servings)

3/4 cup (69 g) sliced almonds, toasted

1 pint (454 g) cherry tomatoes

1/2 cup (12 g) packed basil leaves

1/2 cup (50 g) finely grated
Parmesan cheese

2 Tablespoons (18 g) golden raisins

2 Tablespoons (17 g) capers, drained

1/4 teaspoon crushed red pepper flakes

3 anchovy filets in oil, drained

2 garlic cloves, peeled

1 large jalapeño, 1 1/2 ounces (43 g), seeded

1/2 teaspoon kosher salt

1/8 teaspoon ground black pepper

6 Tablespoons (90 ml) extra virgin olive oil

1. Toast almonds over medium heat in a dry skillet. Toss or stir frequently to prevent burning. Toast until the almonds are a light golden brown, 5 to 7 minutes. Set aside.

2. Place tomatoes into the Vitamix container and secure lid.

3. Select Variable 3.

4. Pulse 4 to 5 times. Remove lid and add almonds, basil, parmesan, raisins, capers, red pepper flakes, anchovy filets, garlic, jalapeño, salt, pepper and secure lid.

5. Select Variable 1.

6. Switch machine to Start and remove lid plug. Slowly pour oil in through the lid plug opening. Blend for 30 seconds. Stop and scrape down sides. Blend an additional 10 seconds.

7. Toss with hot cooked pasta, like fusilli or bow ties, or use as a dip.

>> ***nutritional information:*** *Amount Per 2 Tablespoon (30 g) Serving: Calories 60, Total Fat 5g, Saturated Fat 1g, Cholesterol 0mg, Sodium 80mg, Total Carbohydrate 2g, Dietary Fiber 1g, Protein 2g*

note: You can also toast almonds in a 300°F (150°C) oven. Check every 10 minutes to prevent burning.

green curry *sauce*

preparation: 10 minutes • **processing:** 15 seconds • **yield:** 1 1/2 cups (360 ml) (6 servings)

2 teaspoons sesame oil

1/4 cup (24 g) peeled, chopped fresh ginger root

2 garlic cloves, peeled, sliced

1/4 cup (60 ml) dry white wine

1 Tablespoon fresh lime juice

2 teaspoon green curry paste

13 1/2–ounce (403 ml) can coconut milk

1/2 teaspoon fish sauce (preferably Nam Pla)

1/2 cup (8 g) cilantro leaves

kosher salt, freshly ground black pepper, and lime, to taste

1. In a small saucepan, heat sesame oil over medium heat. Add the ginger and garlic and sauté for 30 seconds. Add the white wine and the lime juice and reduce to almost dry. Add the curry paste, coconut milk and fish sauce and reduce to 1 cup (240 ml) liquid. Let cool 10 minutes.

2. Place the cooked mixture and the cilantro into the Vitamix container and secure lid.

3. Select Variable 1.

4. Switch machine to Start and slowly increase speed to Variable 10.

5. Blend for 15 seconds.

 nutritional information: *Amount Per Serving: Calories 130, Total Fat 12g, Saturated Fat 10g, Cholesterol 0mg, Sodium 100mg, Total Carbohydrate 3g, Dietary Fiber 0g, Protein 1g*

fresh tomato *sauce*

preparation: 15 minutes • **processing:** 20 seconds • **cook time:** 35–40 minutes
yield: 3 1/2 cups (840 ml) (7 servings)

6 medium Roma tomatoes,
(400 g), quartered

1/4 cup (40 g) chopped onion

1/2 cup (65 g) chopped carrot

2 Tablespoons (30 g) tomato paste

1 garlic clove, peeled

1/2 teaspoon dried basil

1/2 teaspoon dried oregano

1/2 teaspoon fresh lemon juice

1/2 teaspoon brown sugar

1/4 teaspoon salt

1. Place all ingredients into the Vitamix container in the order listed and secure lid.

2. Select Variable 1.

3. Switch machine to Start and slowly increase speed to Variable 10.

4. Blend for 20 seconds.

5. Pour into saucepan and simmer for 35 to 40 minutes. Season to taste with additional salt and pepper if necessary.

>> **nutritional information:** *Amount Per Serving: Calories 25, Total Fat 0g, Saturated Fat 0g, Cholesterol 0mg, Sodium 110mg, Total Carbohydrate 5g, Dietary Fiber 1g, Protein 1g*

homemade *mayonnaise*

preparation: 10 minutes • **processing:** 1 minute 15 seconds • **yield:** 3 1/4 cups (780 ml) (52 servings)

3 large pasteurized eggs

1/4 cup (60 ml) fresh lemon juice

1 1/4 teaspoons dry mustard

1 1/2 teaspoons kosher salt

1 3/4 cups (420 ml) canola oil

1. Place eggs, lemon juice, dry mustard and salt into the Vitamix container in the order listed and secure lid.

2. Select Variable 1.

3. Switch machine to Start and slowly increase speed to Variable 7.

4. Blend for 15 seconds. Remove the lid plug and slowly pour oil in through the lid plug opening until mixture is emulsified, about 1 minute.

5. Stop machine and stir in any oil sitting on top. Refrigerate in a separate container and use within 2 to 4 weeks.

>> **nutritional information:** *Amount Per 1 Tablespoon Serving: Calories 70, Total Fat 8g, Saturated Fat 0.5g, Cholesterol 10mg, Sodium 60mg, Total Carbohydrate 0g, Dietary Fiber 0g, Protein 0g*

dijon mint *glaze*

preparation: 10 minutes • **processing:** 20 – 30 seconds • **yield:** 1 cup (240 ml) (4 servings)

1/2 cup (120 g) Dijon mustard

1/2 cup (120 ml) honey

2 Tablespoons (30 g) prepared horseradish

1/3 cup (30 g) fresh mint leaves

1. Place all ingredients into the Vitamix container in the order listed and secure lid.

2. Select Variable 1.

3. Switch machine to Start and slowly increase speed to Variable 6.

4. Blend for 20 to 30 seconds. Stop and scrape sides with a spatula. Blend an additional 5 seconds.

nutritional information: *Amount Per Serving: Calories 170, Total Fat 0g, Saturated Fat 0g, Cholesterol 0mg, Sodium 750mg, Total Carbohydrate 41g, Dietary Fiber 1g, Protein 0g*

note: A quick and easy way to jazz up a weeknight meal, this glaze is nice with plain grilled steak or roast lamb.

all american
steak *sauce*

preparation: 10 minutes • **processing:** 20–30 seconds
yield: 3 cups (720 ml) (24 servings)

6 Tablespoons (102 g) ketchup

3/4 cup (180 ml) molasses

6 Tablespoons (90 ml) honey

3/4 cup (180 g) Dijon mustard

3/4 cup (180 g) whole grain mustard

3 Tablespoons (45 g) prepared horseradish

1 1/2 teaspoons kosher salt

3/4 teaspoon ground black pepper

1. Place all ingredients into the Vitamix container in the order listed and secure lid.

2. Select Variable 1.

3. Switch machine to Start and slowly increase speed to Variable 10.

4. Blend for 20 to 30 seconds.

nutritional information: *Amount Per 2 Tablespoon (30 ml) Serving: Calories 80, Total Fat 0g, Saturated Fat 0g, Cholesterol 0mg, Sodium 420mg, Total Carbohydrate 18g, Dietary Fiber 0g, Protein 0g*

bright idea

This is great for a steak-and-chops barbeque party, or try mixing it with ground beef for barbeque burgers. Double the recipe and freeze half for future use.

fresh *applesauce*

preparation: 10 minutes • **processing:** 20–25 seconds • **yield:** 2 cups (480 ml) (4 servings)

4 medium apples, 1 1/2 pounds (680 g), cored, quartered

2 Tablespoons (30 ml) fresh lemon juice

1. Place all ingredients into the Vitamix container in the order listed and secure lid.
2. Select Variable 1.
3. Switch machine to Start and slowly increase speed to Variable 5.
4. Blend for 20 to 25 seconds.

nutritional information: *Amount Per Serving: Calories 90, Total Fat 0g, Saturated Fat 0g, Cholesterol 0mg, Sodium 0mg, Total Carbohydrate 24g, Dietary Fiber 4g, Protein 0g*

note: For a puréed consistency, increase speed to Variable 4 and blend for 20 seconds.

pineapple *chili* sambal

on the menu

Sambal is an Asian condiment that pairs well with shrimp, fish, and as an enhancer to white rice or grilled meats.

preparation: 20 minutes • **processing:** Pulsing
yield: 2 3/4 cups (660 ml) (132 servings)

2 cups (330 g) fresh pineapple chunks

1/2 cup (8 g) cilantro leaves

3 Tablespoons (45 g) chile paste

3 Tablespoons (45 g) fresh ginger root

6 Tablespoons (90 g) white miso paste

6 Tablespoons (90 ml) rice wine vinegar

1/4 cup (55 g) light brown sugar

2 teaspoons toasted sesame oil

1. Place all ingredients into the Vitamix container in the order listed and secure lid.

2. Select Variable 7.

3. Pulse 5 times or until desired consistency is reached.

4. Store in the refrigerator for up to 1 month.

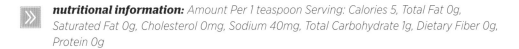 **nutritional information:** *Amount Per 1 teaspoon Serving: Calories 5, Total Fat 0g, Saturated Fat 0g, Cholesterol 0mg, Sodium 40mg, Total Carbohydrate 1g, Dietary Fiber 0g, Protein 0g*

note: This is extremely spicy. Use 1/2–1 teaspoon at a time. If consistency is too thin, add more pineapple chunks to thicken.

parsley *pesto*

preparation: 15 minutes • **processing:** 20–30 seconds • **yield:** 1 1/2 cups (360 ml) (12 servings)

1 cup (240 ml) extra virgin olive oil

1 cup (61 g) packed parsley leaves

2/3 cup (92 g) capers, drained

1 Tablespoon packed fresh oregano leaves

1 Tablespoon white wine vinegar

1/2 teaspoon crushed red pepper flakes

2 garlic cloves, peeled

ground black pepper to taste

1. Place all ingredients into the Vitamix container in the order listed and secure lid.
2. Select Variable 1.
3. Switch machine to Start and slowly increase speed to Variable 5.
4. Blend for 20 to 30 seconds.
5. Serve with grilled vegetables, chicken, or toss with hot cooked pasta.

 **nutritional information:** *Amount Per 2 Tablespoon (30 g) Serving: Calories 170, Total Fat 19g, Saturated Fat 2.5g, Cholesterol 0mg, Sodium 230mg, Total Carbohydrate 1g, Dietary Fiber 0g, Protein 0g*

red pepper dijon
steak *sauce*

preparation: 55 minutes (includes roasting peppers)
processing: 25–30 seconds
yield: 3 1/4 cups (480 ml) (26 servings)

3 red bell peppers, 22 ounces (625 g), roasted, peeled, seeded

3/4 cup (180 ml) sherry vinegar

4 1/2 Tablespoons (68 g) Dijon mustard

3 Tablespoons (45 g) prepared horseradish

3 Tablespoons (45 ml) honey

1 1/2 Tablespoons molasses

3 teaspoons Worcestershire sauce

1 1/2 teaspoons kosher salt

3/4 teaspoon ground black pepper

roasting peppers

Roasted peppers are used in a variety of sauces, salads, and sandwiches to add a deep, rich flavor. Heat oven to broil. Wash and dry peppers, slice them in half, and remove seeds. Place them on foil or a cookie sheet, skin side up. Allow peppers to broil until skin bubbles and wrinkles (about 5–20 minutes, depending on size of the pepper).

1. Place all ingredients into the Vitamix container in the order listed and secure lid.

2. Select Variable 1.

3. Switch machine to Start and slowly increase speed to Variable 7.

4. Blend for 20 to 30 seconds.

nutritional information: *Amount Per 2 Tablespoon (30 ml) Serving: Calories 20, Total Fat 0g, Saturated Fat 0g, Cholesterol 0mg, Sodium 190mg, Total Carbohydrate 5g, Dietary Fiber 1g, Protein 0g*

pesto *mayonnaise*

preparation: 15 minutes • ***processing:*** 2 minutes • ***yield:*** 2 1/2 cups (600 ml) (40 servings)

1/4 cup (60 ml) fresh lemon juice

1 Tablespoon Dijon mustard

3 large egg yolks

4 garlic cloves, peeled

1 teaspoon kosher salt

1 1/4 cups (300 ml) extra virgin olive oil

1 cup (24 g) packed basil leaves

1 cup (60 g) packed parsley leaves

1/4 cup (34 g) pine nuts

1. Place lemon juice, mustard, egg yolks, garlic and salt into the Vitamix container in the order listed and secure lid.

2. Select Variable 1.

3. Switch machine to Start and slowly increase speed to Variable 5.

4. Remove the lid plug and slowly pour oil through the lid plug opening until mixture is emulsified.

5. Stop machine and remove lid. Add basil, parsley, and pine nuts to the Vitamix container and secure lid.

6. Select Variable 1.

7. Switch machine to Start and slowly increase speed to Variable 6.

8. Blend for 20 seconds until smooth.

nutritional information: *Amount Per 1 Tablespoon Serving: Calories 70, Total Fat 8g, Saturated Fat 1g, Cholesterol 15mg, Sodium 60mg, Total Carbohydrate 1g, Dietary Fiber 0g, Protein 0g*

note: This is delicious as a sandwich spread or as a dip for calamari.

tomatillo and pineapple *sauce*

preparation: 25 minutes • ***processing:*** 30 seconds plus Pulsing • ***cook time:*** 1 hour 20 minutes
yield: 4 cups (960 ml) (8 servings)

1 pound (454 g) tomatillos, husked, rinsed

3 ounces (85 g) jalapeños, seeded

4 Tablespoons (56 g) unsalted butter

1 pound (454 g) fresh pineapple, cut into large chunks, core included

1 teaspoon cumin seeds

1/2 teaspoon ground cinnamon

7 1/2 ounce (213 g) Granny Smith apple, cored, halved

2 garlic cloves, peeled

2 Tablespoons (30 ml) olive oil

1/4 cup (60 ml) mango nectar

1 Tablespoon apple cider vinegar

1 Tablespoon granulated sugar

1. Bring a 4-quart saucepan of water to a boil and add tomatillos and jalapeños. Cook until tender, about 10 minutes. Drain.

2. Heat butter in a 12-inch (30 cm) skillet over high heat. Add pineapple, cumin, cinnamon and apple. Cook stirring constantly until beginning to caramelize, about 5 minutes. Reduce heat to medium-low and cook stirring frequently until fruit is tender, about 20 minutes. Remove from heat and add 1/2 cup (120 ml) water, scraping up any brown bits.

3. Place into the Vitamix container and secure lid.

4. Select Variable 1.

5. Switch machine to Start and slowly increase speed to Variable 7.

6. Blend for 30 seconds. Stop machine.

7. Add tomatillos and jalapeños to the Vitamix container and secure lid.

8. Pulse 7 to 8 times until slightly chunky. Set aside.

9. Heat oil in a 6-quart saucepan over high heat; add salsa and 1/2 cup (120 ml) water. Bring to a boil. Reduce heat to low and cook, stirring until thickened, about 45 minutes.

10. Add mango nectar, vinegar and sugar and cook for 1 minute. Remove from heat and let cool before serving.

>> **nutritional information:** *Amount Per Serving: Calories 160, Total Fat 10g, Saturated Fat 4g, Cholesterol 15mg, Sodium 0mg, Total Carbohydrate 18g, Dietary Fiber 2g, Protein 1g*

note: Serve with fish or pork.

kale and basil *pesto*

preparation: 15 minutes • ***processing:*** 20–30 seconds • ***yield:*** 1 3/4 cups (420 g) (14 servings)

1 cup (240 ml) olive oil

1 cup (100 g) grated Parmesan cheese

3 medium garlic cloves, peeled

2 cups (80 g) fresh basil leaves

2 cups (135 g) fresh kale leaves

3 Tablespoons (25 g) pine nuts

1/4 teaspoon kosher salt

pinch ground black pepper

1. Place all ingredients into the Vitamix container in the order listed and secure lid.

2. Select Variable 1.

3. Switch machine to Start and slowly increase speed to Variable 5.

4. Blend for 20 to 30 seconds or until desired consistency is reached.

nutritional information: *Amount Per 2 Tablespoon (30 g) Serving: Calories 190, Total Fat 19g, Saturated Fat 3.5g, Cholesterol 5mg, Sodium 125mg, Total Carbohydrate 2g, Dietary Fiber 0g, Protein 3g*

note: For a classic pesto, omit the kale and increase basil leaves to 4 cups (160 g).

easy *aioli*

preparation: 10 minutes • *processing:* 1 minute • *yield:* 1 3/4 cups (420 g) (28 servings)

3 large pasteurized egg yolks

1/4 cup (60 ml) fresh lemon juice

1 teaspoon salt

1/8 teaspoon ground white pepper

3 large garlic cloves, peeled

1 1/2 cups (360 ml) light olive oil

1. Place egg yolks, lemon juice, salt, pepper and garlic into the Vitamix container in the order listed and secure lid.

2. Select Variable 1.

3. Switch machine to Start and slowly increase speed to Variable 5. Remove the lid plug.

4. While machine is running, slowly pour oil through the lid plug opening. As mixture begins to thicken, the oil may be added at a faster rate. Process should take no longer than 1 minute.

5. Refrigerate in an airtight container.

> *nutritional information:* Amount Per 1 Tablespoon Serving: Calories 110, Total Fat 12g, Saturated Fat 2g, Cholesterol 20mg, Sodium 85mg, Total Carbohydrate 0g, Dietary Fiber 0g, Protein 0g

note: Aioli is a garlic mayonnaise that can be used as a dip or as a sandwich spread.

almond cream *sauce*

preparation: 15 minutes • **processing:** 30 seconds
yield: 2 cups (480 ml) (8 servings)

2 cups (480 ml) unsweetened almond milk

1/2 cup (120 ml) chicken broth

3 1/2 ounces (100 g) fresh
New Mexico green chile peppers

3 scallions, white parts only

3 Tablespoons (20 g) slivered almonds, toasted

1 garlic clove, peeled

1/4 teaspoon salt

1/4 cup (60 ml) heavy cream

on the menu

Brown 1 1/2 pounds (680 g) chicken in canola oil for a few minutes on each side. Pour Almond Cream Sauce into the pan with the chicken and cook over low heat until internal temperature of the chicken reaches 180°F (80°C). Serve over fettucine.

⚠ **CAUTION**

Contents Will Be Hot.

1. Combine almond milk, chicken broth, chilies, scallion, almonds, garlic, and salt in a medium saucepan; bring to a boil. Reduce heat to a simmer and cook until the mixture is reduced by half, 30 minutes.

2. Place mixture into the Vitamix container and secure lid.

3. Select Variable 1.

4. Switch machine to Start and slowly increase speed to Variable 5.

5. Blend for 15 seconds. Reduce speed to Variable 1 and remove the lid plug. Add heavy cream through the lid plug opening.

6. Blend for an additional 15 seconds.

nutritional information: *Amount Per Serving: Calories 60, Total Fat 5g, Saturated Fat 2g, Cholesterol 10mg, Sodium 180mg, Total Carbohydrate 3g, Dietary Fiber 1g, Protein 1g*

chunky apple cranberry *sauce*

preparation: 20 minutes • ***processing:*** Pulsing • ***cook time:*** 20 minutes
yield: 2 cups (480 ml) (8 servings)

3 Tablespoons (45 g) butter

2 cups (230 g) sliced red onion

3/4 cup (180 ml) apple juice

1/2 cup (120 ml) orange juice

2–3 teaspoons adobo sauce from canned chipotle chilies (optional)

7 1/2 ounce (213 g) apple, cut into large chunks

1/2 cup (55 g) fresh or frozen cranberries

1. Melt butter in a large skillet. Add onion and sauté over medium heat until lightly browned, 7 minutes.

2. Add juices, apples, cranberries and adobo sauce, if using. Bring to a boil; simmer for 10 minutes.

3. Place mixture into the Vitamix container and secure lid.

4. Select Variable 6.

5. Pulse 6 times until combined.

 nutritional information: *Amount Per Serving: Calories 80, Total Fat 4.5g, Saturated Fat 3g, Cholesterol 10mg, Sodium 40mg, Total Carbohydrate 12g, Dietary Fiber 1g, Protein 1g*

note: This is a good condiment with poultry. If using the adobo sauce, the flavor goes well with pork.

⚠ **CAUTION**

Contents Will Be Hot.

spicy mango *sauce*

preparation: 15 minutes • **processing:** 15 seconds • **cook time:** 10 – 15 minutes
yield: 1 3/4 cups (420 ml) (14 servings)

2 Tablespoons (30 ml) canola oil

2 1/2 ounce (71 g) onion, rough chopped

5 1/2 ounce (156 g) red bell pepper, seeded, rough chopped

3 1/2 ounce (100 g) tomato, rough chopped

3/4 cup (180 g) hot mango chutney

1. Heat oil in a medium-size saucepan over medium heat. Add onion and bell pepper, cover, and cook 5 to 7 minutes. Add tomato, cover, and cook 5 to 7 minutes. Add chutney, stirring to heat through. Cook for 1 to 2 minutes.

2. Place mixture into the Vitamix container and secure lid.

3. Select Variable 1.

4. Switch machine to Start and slowly increase speed to Variable 5.

5. Blend for 15 seconds.

6. Serve warm with grilled tofu or fish.

 nutritional information: *Amount Per 2 Tablespoon (30 ml) Serving: Calories 60, Total Fat 3.5g, Saturated Fat 0g, Cholesterol 0mg, Sodium 140mg, Total Carbohydrate 8g, Dietary Fiber 1g, Protein 0g*

desserts

desserts

baked desserts • fondue • frozen treats • toppings

taste of summer peach soy *sherbet*

preparation: 10 minutes • ***processing:*** 55 seconds • ***yield:*** 5 cups (1.2 l) (10 servings)

1 1/2 cups (340 g) vanilla soy yogurt

3–5 Tablespoons (30 g) powdered sugar

1 teaspoon vanilla extract

1 1/2 pounds (680 g) frozen unsweetened peach slices

1. Place all ingredients into the Vitamix container in the order listed and secure lid.

2. Select Variable 1.

3. Switch machine to Start. Use the tamper to press the ingredients into the blades.

4. In about 55 seconds, the sound of the motor will change and four mounds should form.

5. Stop machine. Do not overmix or melting will occur. Serve immediately.

>> **nutritional information:** *Amount Per 1/2 Cup (120g) Serving: Calories 60, Total Fat .5g, Saturated Fat 0g, Cholesterol 0mg, Sodium 0mg, Total Carbohydrate 14g, Dietary Fiber 2g, Protein 1g*

note: Soften peaches in a large bowl for 20 minutes at room temperature before blending.

mini almond *macaroons*

preparation: 10 minutes • **processing:** Pulsing • **bake time:** 12-15 minutes
yield: 25 small macaroons

6 ounces (170 g) almond paste

6 Tablespoons (75 g) plus 2 teaspoons granulated sugar

2 large egg whites

1. Line a baking sheet with parchment paper. Preheat oven to 325°F (160°C).

2. Place almond paste and sugar into the Vitamix container and secure lid.

3. Select Variable 7.

4. Pulse 10 times to combine. Add egg white. Pulse an additional 10 times. Stop and scrape sides, continuing to pulse until blended.

5. Place batter in a medium size pastry bag fitted with a small round tip.

6. Pipe batter into small circles on prepared baking sheet.

7. Bake 12 to 15 minutes until they begin to brown on the edges. Cool and then loosen with a spatula.

>> **nutritional information:** *Amount Per Macaroon: Calories 50, Total Fat 1.5g, Saturated Fat 0g, Cholesterol 0mg, Sodium 0mg, Total Carbohydrate 7g, Dietary Fiber 0g, Protein 1g*

strawberry grand marnier *sorbet*

preparation: 10 minutes • **processing:** 45–55 seconds • **yield:** 3 cups (720 ml) (6 servings)

1 cup (240 ml) orange juice

4 ounces (120 ml) Grand Marnier

1/2 pound (227 g) frozen pineapple chunks

1 1/2 pound (680 g) frozen unsweetened strawberries

1. Place all ingredients into the Vitamix container in the order listed and secure lid.

2. Select Variable 1.

3. Switch machine to Start and slowly increase speed to Variable 10, using the tamper to press ingredients into the blades.

4. In about 45 to 55 seconds, the sound of the motor will change and four mounds should form.

5. Stop machine. Do not over mix or melting will occur. Serve immediately.

nutritional information: *Amount Per Serving: Calories 70, Total Fat 0g, Saturated Fat 0g, Cholesterol 0mg, Sodium 0mg, Total Carbohydrate 12g, Dietary Fiber 2g, Protein 1g*

note: For best results, allow frozen fruit to thaw at room temperature for 10 minutes before blending.

chocolate orange *fondue*

preparation: 20 minutes • **processing:** 2 minutes 10 seconds • **yield:** 2 1/4 cups (540 ml) (18 servings)

1 cup (240 ml) heavy whipping cream

2 teaspoons grated orange peel

8 ounces (227 g) semi-sweet baking chocolate, chopped

3 Tablespoons (45 ml) Grand Marnier

1. Place cream, orange peel and chocolate into the Vitamix container in the order listed and secure lid.

2. Select Variable 1.

3. Switch machine to Start and slowly increase speed to Variable 10.

4. Blend for 4 minutes 30 seconds.

5. Reduce speed to Variable 1 and remove the lid plug. Drizzle the Grand Marnier through the lid plug opening. Blend an additional 10 seconds.

6. Pour into a fondue pot and serve.

nutritional information: *Amount Per 2 Tablespoon (29g) Serving: Calories 130, Total Fat 10g, Saturated Fat 6g, Cholesterol 10mg, Sodium 5mg, Total Carbohydrate 8g, Dietary Fiber 6g, Protein 1g*

note: For dippers, try sponge cake, pound cake, sliced apples, sliced pears, marshmallows, graham crackers, strawberries, bananas, fresh or canned pineapple chunks.

strawberry yogurt *freeze*

preparation: 10 minutes • ***processing:*** 45–55 seconds • ***yield:*** 5 cups (1.2 l) (10 servings)

1 1/2 cups (360 g) low-fat vanilla yogurt

1 1/2 pounds (680 g) frozen unsweetened strawberries

1. Place all ingredients into the Vitamix container in the order listed and secure lid.

2. Select Variable 1.

3. Switch machine to Start and slowly increase speed to Variable 10, using the tamper to press ingredients into the blades.

4. In about 45 to 55 seconds, the sound of the motor will change and four mounds should form in the mixture.

5. Stop machine. Do not over mix or melting will occur. Serve immediately.

>> ***nutritional information:*** *Amount Per Serving: Calories 50, Total Fat 0g, Saturated Fat 0g, Cholesterol 0mg, Sodium 25mg, Total Carbohydrate 11g, Dietary Fiber 1g, Protein 2g*

low-fat pumpkin *pie*

preparation: 15 minutes • **processing:** 10–15 seconds
bake time: 1 hour • **yield:** 3 pies (24 slices)

1 cup (240 g) egg substitute

3 1/2 cups (850 g) canned pumpkin

1 1/2 cups (300 g) granulated sugar

1 teaspoon salt

2 teaspoons ground cinnamon

1 teaspoon ground ginger

1/2 teaspoon ground cloves

3 cups (720 ml) evaporated nonfat milk

3 unbaked 9–inch (23 cm) deep-dish pie shells

whipped topping

1. Preheat oven to 425°F (220°C).

2. Place egg substitute, pumpkin, sugar, salt, cinnamon, ginger, cloves and evaporated milk into the Vitamix container in the order listed and secure lid.

3. Select Variable 1.

4. Switch machine to Start and slowly increase speed to Variable 5.

5. Blend for 10 to 15 seconds.

6. Pour into 3 unbaked 9–inch (23 cm) deep-dish pie shells.

7. Bake for 15 minutes. Reduce oven temperature to 350°F (180°C). Bake for 40 minutes. Pie is done when knife inserted into center comes out clean. Filling will be soft, but firms up as it sets and cools.

8. Chill and serve topped with whipped topping.

 **nutritional information:** *Amount Per Slice: Calories 220, Total Fat 8g, Saturated Fat 2.5g, Cholesterol 0mg, Sodium 250mg, Total Carbohydrate 32g, Dietary Fiber 2g, Protein 5g*

fruity versatility

Strawberry Yogurt Freeze is delicious with any frozen fruit or your favorite berry blend. Try swapping out the strawberries for blueberries, blackberries, or even a peach-mango combination. After dark, add drama with a birthday candle and a mint leaf placed on each serving.

cookies and cream *freeze*

preparation: 10 minutes • **processing:** Pulsing • **yield:** 2 cups (480 ml) (4 servings)

2 1/2 cups (340 g) vanilla ice cream

1 ounce (30 ml) chocolate syrup

6 chocolate sandwich cookies, divided use

1 ounce (30 g) white chocolate

1. Place ice cream, syrup, 4 cookies and white chocolate into the Vitamix container in the order listed and secure lid.

2. Select Variable 8.

3. Pulse 18 to 20 times, using the tamper to press the ingredients into the blades.

4. Add remaining cookies and Pulse 6 times to incorporate.

» *nutritional information:* Amount Per Serving: Calories 320, Total Fat 17g, Saturated Fat 8g, Cholesterol 35mg, Sodium 150mg, Total Carbohydrate 39g, Dietary Fiber 1g, Protein 5g

herbed apple *granita*

preparation: 10 minutes • **processing:** 1 1/2 minutes
yield: 4 cups (960 ml) (8 servings)

3 cups (720 ml) apple juice

4 teaspoons fresh lemon juice

1/2 cup (100 g) granulated sugar

1/2 cup (48 g) fresh tarragon leaves

frozen treats

This light and simple treat is great for all occasions and can easily be made ahead. Simply portion the mixture into dessert dishes and keep in the freezer until you're ready to serve. Use granitas as a stand-alone dessert or to cleanse the palate between courses of a formal meal.

1. Place all ingredients into the Vitamix container in the order listed and secure lid.

2. Select Variable 1.

3. Switch machine to Start and slowly increase speed to Variable 10.

4. Blend for 20 to 30 seconds.

5. Pour into two standard ice cube trays and freeze until solid, about 4 hours. Let trays thaw at room temperature for 10 minutes.

6. Place ice cubes into the Vitamix container and secure lid.

7. Select Variable 1.

8. Switch machine to Start and slowly increase speed to Variable 10.

9. Blend for 20 to 30 seconds, using the tamper to press the ice cubes into the blades. As mixture begins to freeze, the sound of the motor will change and the mixture will start to flow through the blades. Toward the end of processing, leave tamper in to encourage formation of four mounds.

nutritional information: *Amount Per Serving: Calories 90, Total Fat 0g, Saturated Fat 0g, Cholesterol 0mg, Sodium 10mg, Total Carbohydrate 24g, Dietary Fiber 0g, Protein 0g*

brown sugar surprise *cupcakes*

preparation: 20 minutes • ***processing:*** 30 seconds • ***bake time:*** 20–25 minutes
yield: 24 full size cupcakes

1 1/4 cups (300 ml) milk

2 large eggs

1 1/2 teaspoons vanilla extract

2/3 cup (150 g) unsalted butter, softened

1 3/4 cups (350 g) granulated sugar

2 1/2 cups (312 g) all-purpose flour

2 1/2 teaspoons baking powder

1/2 teaspoon salt

1/2 cup (110 g) packed brown sugar

1/4 cup (27 g) finely chopped pecans

1 teaspoon ground cinnamon

1. Line 24 2 1/2–inch (6 cm) muffin cups with paper baking cups. Preheat oven to 350°F (180°C).

2. Place milk, eggs, vanilla, butter and sugar into the Vitamix container in the order listed and secure lid.

3. Select Variable 1.

4. Switch machine to Start and slowly increase speed to Variable 7.

5. Blend for 30 seconds.

6. In a large-size mixing bowl, combine flour, baking powder and salt.

7. Pour wet ingredients into the dry ingredients and mix by hand to combine.

8. In a small bowl, whisk together brown sugar, pecans and cinnamon.

9. Spoon 1 Tablespoon of batter into each prepared muffin cup. Sprinkle 1 teaspoon of the brown sugar mixture over batter in cups. Spoon remaining batter evenly over brown sugar mixture in each cup. Sprinkle remaining brown sugar mixture over batter in cups.

10. Bake for 20 to 25 minutes, or until a toothpick inserted in centers comes out clean. Cool on wire racks for 10 minutes. Remove cupcakes from muffin cups and cool completely.

11. Top with 2 Tablespoons (30 g) Creamy Butter Frosting.

>> ***nutritional information:*** *Amount Per Cupcake: Calories 190, Total Fat 7g, Saturated Fat 3.5g, Cholesterol 30mg, Sodium 115mg, Total Carbohydrate 30g, Dietary Fiber 1g, Protein 2g*

orange *sorbet*

preparation: 10 minutes • **processing:** 45–55 seconds • **yield:** 3 cups (720 ml) (6 servings)

2 oranges, peeled, halved

1 Tablespoon orange juice concentrate

1 teaspoon orange zest

2 Tablespoons (25 g) granulated sugar

4 cups (960 ml) ice cubes

1. Place all ingredients into the Vitamix container in the order listed and secure lid.

2. Select Variable 1.

3. Switch machine to Start and slowly increase speed to Variable 10, using the tamper to press ingredients into the blades.

4. In about 45 to 55 seconds, the sound of the motor will change and four mounds should form.

5. Stop machine. Do not over mix or melting will occur. Serve immediately

>> **nutritional information:** *Amount Per Serving: Calories 40, Saturated Fat 0g, Cholesterol 0mg, Sodium 0mg, Total Carbohydrate 11g, Dietary Fiber 1g, Protein 0g*

vegan raisin almond *cookies*

fancy finishes

It's easy to dress up these buttery Almond cookies for a special occasion. Press a roasted almond into the center of each cookie after removing from the oven.

preparation: 20 minutes • **processing:** 45 seconds
bake time: 14 minutes • **yield:** 44 cookies

3/4 cup (180 ml) cold, strong coffee

1/4 cup (56 g) vegan margarine, melted and cooled

1 teaspoon almond extract

1/2 cup (80 g) pitted prunes

1 1/3 cups (267 g) granulated sugar

1 Tablespoon flax seeds

2 1/4 cups (280 g) all-purpose flour

3/4 teaspoon baking powder

3/4 teaspoon baking soda

1/4 teaspoon salt

3/4 cup (120 g) golden raisins

1/2 cup (72 g) chopped almonds

1. Line a baking sheet with silpat or parchment paper. Preheat oven to 375°F (190°C).

2. Place coffee, melted margarine, almond extract, prunes, sugar and flaxseeds into the Vitamix container in the order listed and secure lid.

3. Select Variable 1.

4. Switch machine to Start and slowly increase speed to Variable 10.

5. Blend for 30 seconds.

6. Place flour, baking powder, baking soda and salt into a medium-size mixing bowl. Stir by hand to combine.

7. Pour wet mixture into dry mixture and mix by hand to combine. Stir in raisins and almonds.

8. Drop by rounded Tablespoons onto prepared baking sheet.

9. Bake for 14 minutes. Transfer to wire rack to cool.

 nutritional information: *Amount Per Cookie: Calories 80, Total Fat 2g, Saturated Fat 0g, Cholesterol 0mg, Sodium 65mg, Total Carbohydrate 15g, Dietary Fiber 1g, Protein 1g*

mixed spice berry *sorbet*

preparation: 25 minutes • **processing:** 1 minute 15 seconds • **yield:** 4 1/4 cups (1.0 l) (9 servings)

1/2 ounce (14 g) fresh ginger root, peeled

1 cup (240 ml) cold water

1/2 cup (100 g) granulated sugar

1 cup (150 g) frozen unsweetened strawberries

1 cup (140 g) frozen unsweetened blueberries

1 cup (140 g) frozen unsweetened blackberries

1 cup (140 g) frozen unsweetened red raspberries

2 cups (300 g) frozen pitted Bing cherries

1/2 cup (13 g) fresh mint leaves

1/8 teaspoon ground cloves

1/8 teaspoon ground allspice

1/4 teaspoon ground nutmeg

1/2 teaspoon ground cinnamon

1 teaspoon vanilla extract

1. Partially thaw frozen berries for 20 minutes; set aside.

2. Place ginger, water and sugar into the Vitamix container and secure lid.

3. Select Variable 1.

4. Switch machine to Start and slowly increase speed to Variable 10.

5. Blend for 20 seconds until ginger is finely chopped. Stop machine and remove lid. Add berries, mint, cloves, allspice, nutmeg, cinnamon and vanilla to the container with ginger mixture and secure lid.

6. Select Variable 1.

7. Switch machine to Start and slowly increase speed to Variable 10, using the tamper to press the ingredients into the blades. In about 45 to 55 seconds, the sound of the motor will change and four mounds should form.

8. Stop machine. Do not over mix or melting will occur. Serve immediately.

>> **nutritional information:** *Amount Per Serving: Calories 90, Total Fat 0g, Saturated Fat 0g, Cholesterol 0mg, Sodium 0mg, Total Carbohydrate 24g, Dietary Fiber 3g, Protein 1g*

whipped cream

preparation: 10 minutes • **processing:** 45 seconds–1 minute • **yield:** 2 cups (480 ml) (16 servings)

2 cups (480 ml) heavy whipping cream, cold

1. Place cream into the Vitamix container and secure lid.

2. Select Variable 1.

3. Switch machine to Start and slowly increase speed to Variable 10.

4. Blend for 45 seconds to 1 minute or until cream becomes firm and whipped.

>> **nutritional information:** *Amount Per 2 Tablespoon (30 g) Serving: Calories 100, Total Fat 11g, Saturated Fat 7g, Cholesterol 40mg, Sodium 10mg, Total Carbohydrate 1g, Dietary Fiber 0g, Protein 1g*

powdered sugar

preparation: 10 minutes • **processing:** 40 seconds • **yield:** 2 cups (480 ml) (96 servings)

1 1/2 cups (300 g) granulated sugar

1 Tablespoon cornstarch

1. Place sugar into the Vitamix container and secure lid.

2. Select Variable 1.

3. Switch machine to Start and slowly increase speed to Variable 10.

4. Blend for 30 seconds. Reduce speed to Variable 3 and remove the lid plug.

5. Add in cornstarch through the lid plug opening and replace lid plug.

6. Slowly increase speed to Variable 10. Blend an additional 10 seconds.

 **nutritional information:** *Amount Per 1 teaspoon Serving: Calories 15, Total Fat 0g, Saturated Fat 0g, Cholesterol 0mg, Sodium 0mg, Total Carbohydrate 3g, Dietary Fiber 0g, Protein 0g*

note: Adding cornstarch to powdered sugar prevents the sugar from caking and improves flow. If using immediately, cornstarch is optional.

creamy butter *frosting*

---

preparation: 30 minutes • **processing:** Pulsing
yield: 4 cups (960 ml) (32 servings)

1/2 cup (114 g) unsalted butter, softened at room temperature for 30 minutes

1 teaspoon vanilla extract

dash salt

4 cups (590 g) powdered sugar

1/4 cup (60 ml) whipping cream

2–4 Tablespoons (30–60 ml) water

1. Place all ingredients into the Vitamix container in the order listed and secure lid.

2. Select Variable 6.

3. Pulse 30 to 60 times, stopping to scrape down sides until well blended, adding additional water if needed.

 **nutritional information:** *Amount Per 2 Tablespoon (22 g) Serving: Calories 90, Total Fat 3.5g, Saturated Fat 2.5g, Cholesterol 10mg, Sodium 0mg, Total Carbohydrate 15g, Dietary Fiber 0g, Protein 0g*

looking good

Use this delicious frosting on a number of breads and desserts, such as Carrot Raisin Muffins (Breakfasts) and Brown Sugar Surprise Cupcakes (Desserts).
Add food coloring for a traditional holiday sugar cookie frosting.

raisin almond *cheesecake*

preparation: 20 minutes • **processing:** 20 seconds plus Pulsing • **bake time:** 1 hour
yield: 12 servings

3/4 cup (94 g) all-purpose flour

2 Tablespoons (25 g) granulated sugar

1/8 teaspoon salt

1/3 cup (75 g) unsalted butter

2 1/2 cups (620 g) ricotta cheese

1/2 cup (100 g) granulated sugar

3 Tablespoons (23 g) all-purpose flour

3 large eggs

1 Tablespoon orange zest

1 Tablespoon lemon zest

1 teaspoon vanilla extract

1/4 teaspoon salt

2 Tablespoons (20 g) golden raisins or chopped, dried cherries

2 Tablespoons (18 g) chopped almonds

1. Preheat oven to 475°F (250°C). Spray the bottom of a 9–inch (23 cm) spring-form pan well with cooking spray.

2. Place flour, sugar, salt and butter into the Vitamix container and secure lid.

3. Select Variable 6.

4. Pulse 4 times until coarsely combined. Press mixture into the bottom of spring-form pan.

5. Bake for 10 minute or until light golden on top. Cool on wire rack. Reduce heat to 350°F (180°C).

6. Place ricotta cheese, sugar, flour, eggs, orange zest, vanilla and salt into the Vitamix container and secure lid.

7. Select Variable 3.

8. Switch machine to Start and blend for 15 seconds. Stop and scrape down sides of container with a spatula. Blend an additional 5 seconds.

9. Pour into a bowl. Stir in raisins, lemon zest and almonds.

10. Pour mixture over crust. Bake for 50 minutes or until center is set.

11. Run a knife around edge of cheesecake to loosen. Let cool completely on a wire rack. Cover and chill 8 hours.

>> **nutritional information:** *Amount Per Serving: Calories 210, Total Fat 14g, Saturated Fat 8g, Cholesterol 85mg, Sodium 135mg, Total Carbohydrate 13g, Dietary Fiber 1g, Protein 9g*

breakfasts

breakfasts

breads • crêpes • eggs • muffins • pancakes • waffle

lemon ginger *muffins*

preparation: 15 minutes • ***processing:*** 30 seconds • ***bake time:*** 15 – 20 minutes
yield: 12 muffins

2 cups plus 2 teaspoons (250 g) all-purpose flour, divided use

1 Tablespoon freshly grated lemon zest plus 2 teaspoons, divided use

1 3/4 teaspoons baking powder

1/4 teaspoon salt

3/4 cup (100 g) granulated sugar, divided use

1/4 cup (60 g) crystallized ginger, small pieces

1/3 cup (75 g) unsalted butter, softened plus 3 Tablespoons (42 g), divided use

1 large egg

3/4 cup (180 ml) milk

1 Tablespoon fresh lemon juice

1. Preheat oven to 350°F (180°C). Spray 12–cup muffin tins with cooking spray; set aside.

2. In a medium-sized mixing bowl mix together flour, 1 Tablespoon lemon zest, baking powder and salt; set aside.

3. Place 1/2 cup (100 g) sugar and crystallized ginger into the Vitamix container and secure lid.

4. Select Variable 1.

5. Switch machine to Start and slowly increase speed to Variable 5.

6. Blend for 5 seconds. Stop machine and remove lid.

7. Add 1/3 cup (75 g) butter to the Vitamix container and secure lid.

8. Select Variable 1.

9. Switch machine to Start and slowly increase speed to Variable 6.

10. Blend for 10 seconds. Stop machine and scrape sides of container with a spatula.

11. Add egg and milk to the Vitamix container and secure lid.

12. Select Variable 1.

13. Switch machine to Start and slowly increase speed to Variable 6.

14. Blend for 15 seconds.

15. Pour wet mixture into dry mixture and combine by hand until well mixed.

16. Spoon 1/4 cup (60 g) batter into each muffin tin.

17. Bake until toothpick inserted in center comes out clean and edges are very lightly browned (15 to 20 minutes).

18. Meanwhile, in small bowl stir together 1/4 cup (50 g) sugar and 2 teaspoons lemon zest; set aside.

19. In small bowl stir together 3 Tablespoons (45 ml) melted butter and lemon juice; set aside.

20. While muffins are still hot, roll tops in melted butter mixture, then in sugar and lemon zest mixture.

21. Place muffins on wire rack to cool.

>> **nutritional information:** *Amount Per Muffin: Calories 230, Total Fat 9g, Saturated Fat 6g, Cholesterol 40mg, Sodium 135mg, Total Carbohydrate 34g, Dietary Fiber 1g, Protein 3g*

whole wheat *crêpes*

preparation: 45 minutes • ***processing:*** 15 seconds • ***cook time:*** 10 minutes • ***yield:*** 14 crêpes

1 cup (120 g) whole wheat flour	6 large eggs
1 cup (125 g) all-purpose flour	4 teaspoons canola oil
1/2 teaspoon salt	2 teaspoons granulated sugar
1 cup (240 ml) 2% milk	1 cup (240 ml) seltzer water

1. Place flours and salt in a medium-size mixing bowl and stir by hand to combine.

2. Place milk, eggs, oil and sugar into the Vitamix container in the order listed and secure lid.

3. Select Variable 1.

4. Switch machine to Start and slowly increase speed to Variable 5.

5. Blend for 15 seconds.

6. Pour wet mixture into dry mixture and use a whisk to combine. Place covered, in the refrigerator for at least 30 minutes.

7. Slowly whisk seltzer water into the batter.

8. Spray a nonstick skillet with cooking spray, heat over medium-high. Ladle 1/3 cup (80 ml) batter onto the center of the pan and immediately tilt and rotate the pan to spread the batter evenly over the bottom.

9. Cook about 30 seconds, until underside is lightly browned. Use a heat resistant spatula to lift the edge of the crêpe and then grab with your fingers to flip. Cook until second side is lightly browned. Slide onto plate. Repeat with remaining batter. Cover crêpes with waxed paper as you prepare the filling.

>> ***nutritional information:*** *Amount Per Crêpe: Calories 120, Total Fat 4g, Saturated Fat 1g, Cholesterol 80mg, Sodium 120mg, Total Carbohydrate 15g, Dietary Fiber 1g, Protein 5g*

coconut *waffles*

preparation: 20 minutes • **processing:** 10 seconds
yield: 7 waffles

1 3/4 cups (220 g) all-purpose flour

2 Tablespoons (25 g) granulated sugar

1 Tablespoon baking powder

3 large eggs

14 ounce (400 ml) can unsweetened light coconut milk

6 Tablespoons (85 g) butter, softened

3/4 cup (60 g) unsweetened shredded coconut

1/2 cup (72 g) almonds, chopped and toasted

toasting almonds

Toast almonds in a dry skillet over medium high heat until deep browned. Toss pan frequently to prevent from burning. Let cool 10 minutes. Place almonds into the Vitamix container and secure lid. Select Variable 5. Pulse 5 times or until chopped.

1. Place flour, sugar and baking powder in a medium-size mixing bowl and stir by hand to combine.

2. Place eggs, coconut milk, butter and coconut into the Vitamix container in the order listed and secure lid.

3. Select Variable 5.

4. Switch machine to Start and blend for 10 seconds.

5. Pour wet mixture into dry mixture and mix by hand to combine.

6. Place 1/2 cup batter onto a preheated waffle maker. Bake according to manufacturer's instructions.

7. Garnish with toasted almonds.

 **nutritional information:** *Amount Per Waffle: Calories 390, Total Fat 26g, Saturated Fat 15g, Cholesterol 105mg, Sodium 340mg, Total Carbohydrate 33g, Dietary Fiber 3g, Protein 9g*

note: For a dessert option, top with a scoop of pineapple sorbet and whipped cream.

cranberry nut *bread*

preparation: 15 minutes • **processing:** 15 seconds • **bake time:** 60 minutes
yield: 1 loaf (16 slices)

1 1/2 teaspoons baking powder

1/2 teaspoon baking soda

1 teaspoon salt

1 cup (120 g) whole wheat flour

1 cup (125 g) all-purpose flour

1 orange, peeled, with 2–inch (5 cm) strip of peel remaining, halved

1/4 cup (60 ml) light olive oil or vegetable oil

3/4 cup (180 ml) milk

1 cup (200 g) granulated sugar

1 large egg

1 cup (100 g) fresh cranberries

1/2 cup (60 g) chopped walnuts

1. Preheat oven to 350°F (180°C). Spray an 8 1/2–inch x 4 1/2–inch (22 cm x 11 cm) loaf pan with cooking spray.

2. Combine baking powder, baking soda, salt and flours in a large-size mixing bowl. Set aside.

3. Place orange, oil, milk, sugar and egg into the Vitamix container in the order listed and secure lid.

4. Select Variable 1.

5. Switch machine to Start and slowly increase speed to Variable 10.

6. Blend for 15 seconds.

7. Pour orange juice mixture into the dry ingredients, mixing by hand until ingredients are just moistened.

8. Gently stir in cranberries and chopped walnuts.

9. Spread the batter in the prepared loaf pan.

10. Bake for 60 minutes or until a knife inserted into the center comes out clean.

nutritional information: *Amount Per Slice: Calories 180, Total Fat 7g, Saturated Fat 1g, Cholesterol 15mg, Sodium 240mg, Total Carbohydrate 27g, Dietary Fiber 2g, Protein 3g*

peanut butter and banana *muffins*

preparation: 20 minutes • **processing:** 20 seconds • **bake time:** 20 minutes • **yield:** 24 muffins

3 cups (375 g) all-purpose flour

1 Tablespoon baking powder

1/4 teaspoon salt

3/4 cup (180 ml) 2% milk

2 large eggs

1 Tablespoon vanilla extract

2 ripe medium bananas, peeled

3/4 cup (192 g) peanut butter

1/3 cup (70 g) unsalted butter, softened

1 1/2 cups (300 g) granulated sugar

1/3 cup (27 g) rolled oats

1. Preheat oven to 400°F (200°C). Line 24 muffin cups with paper baking cups.

2. Place flour, baking powder and salt in a large-size mixing bowl and stir by hand to combine.

3. Place milk, eggs, vanilla, bananas, peanut butter, butter and sugar into the Vitamix container in the order listed and secure lid.

4. Select Variable 5.

5. Switch machine to Start and blend for 15 seconds.

6. Pour wet mixture into dry mixture and mix by hand to combine.

7. Spoon into lined muffin cups. Sprinkle oats over batter. Bake 20 minute or until toothpick inserted in center comes out clean. Cool on wire racks.

》 **nutritional information:** *Amount Per Muffin: Calories 150, Total Fat 2.5g, Saturated Fat 0.5g, Cholesterol 15mg, Sodium 110mg, Total Carbohydrate 29g, Dietary Fiber 1g, Protein 4g*

note: Top with strawberry jam for a fun, kid-friendly breakfast.

sweet breakfast *crêpes*

preparation: 15 minutes • **processing:** Pulsing
cook time: 15–20 minutes • **yield:** 6 crêpes

1 1/4 cups (310 g) part-skim ricotta cheese

1 Tablespoon granulated sugar

1/4 teaspoon vanilla extract

6 Tablespoons (34 g) toasted, sliced almonds

6 Tablespoons (120 g) apricot jam

1 Tablespoon water

6 Whole Wheat Crêpes (recipe found in this section)

1. Place ricotta, sugar and vanilla extract into the Vitamix container and secure lid.

2. Select Variable 4.

3. Pulse 3 times. Scrape down sides of container with a spatula and Pulse 2 times.

4. Combine apricot jam water in a small saucepan. Heat on medium until bubbling; remove from heat and let cool.

5. Place crêpe on a clean cutting board or plate. Spread ricotta filling in the center, leaving a 1 to 2-inch (2.5 cm–5 cm) border. Top with 1 Tablespoon of almonds. Fold the right side just past the middle and do the same with the left side. Drizzle with 1 Tablespoon of apricot syrup. Repeat with 5 more crêpes.

 nutritional information: *Amount Per Crêpe: Calories 280, Total Fat 11g, Saturated Fat 4g, Cholesterol 95mg, Sodium 190mg, Total Carbohydrate 33g, Dietary Fiber 2g, Protein 13g*

jammin' flavor

This recipe is delicious with any of your favorite jams. For a change of scenery, replace the apricot with your favorite fruit filling to create a whole new flavor. Then top with Whipped Cream or Powdered Sugar from the Desserts section.

carrot raisin *muffins*

preparation: 20 minutes · **processing:** 30 seconds · **bake time:** 20-25 minutes
yield: 12 muffins

1 2/3 cups (200 g) self-rising flour

1/2 teaspoon baking soda

1 teaspoon ground cinnamon

1 teaspoon pumpkin pie spice

1 cup (165 g) raisins

2/3 cup (160 ml) light olive oil

2 large eggs

3/4 cup (150 g) granulated sugar

3/4 cup (100 g) chopped carrots

1. Preheat the oven to 350°F (180°C). Spray a 12-cup muffin tin with cooking spray or line with paper liners.

2. Place flour, baking soda, cinnamon and pumpkin pie spice in a medium-size mixing bowl and stir lightly. Stir in raisins. Set aside.

3. Place oil, eggs, sugar and carrots into the Vitamix container and secure lid.

4. Select Variable 1.

5. Switch machine to Start and slowly increase speed to Variable 6.

6. Blend for 20 seconds until thick and creamy.

7. Pour carrot mixture into flour mixture and fold by hand to combine. Spoon the mixture into prepared muffin tin.

8. Bake for 20 to 25 minutes until golden brown. Transfer to a wire rack to cool before serving.

>> ***nutritional information:*** *Amount Per Muffin: Calories 270, Total Fat 13g, Saturated Fat 2g, Cholesterol 30mg, Sodium 300mg, Total Carbohydrate 37g, Dietary Fiber 1g, Protein 3g*

note: Substitute 1 2/3 all-purpose flour, 2 teaspoons baking powder, and 1/2 teaspoon salt for the self-rising flour.

multi seed *loaf*

preparation: 30 minutes • **processing:** 15 seconds • **bake time:** 50–55 minutes
yield: 1 loaf (16 slices)

1 1/2 cups (188 g) all-purpose flour

1/2 cup (60 g) whole wheat flour

1 teaspoon baking powder

1 teaspoon baking soda

1/2 teaspoon salt

3/4 cup (165 g) lightly packed brown sugar

1/2 cup (60 g) shelled raw sunflower seeds, lightly toasted

1/3 cup (35 g) flax seed meal

2 Tablespoons (21 g) whole flax seed

2 Tablespoons (19 g) poppy seed

2 Tablespoons (17 g) sesame seed

1 large egg

1 1/4 cups (300 ml) low-fat buttermilk

1/4 cup (60 ml) vegetable oil

1 teaspoon whole flax seed

1 teaspoon sesame seed

1 teaspoon shelled raw sunflower seeds

1. Preheat oven to 350°F (180°C). Spray a 9–inch x 5–inch (23 cm x 13 cm) loaf pan with cooking spray.

2. Place flours, baking powder, baking soda, salt, brown sugar, sunflower seeds, flaxseed meal, whole flaxseed, poppy seed and sesame seed in a large-size mixing bowl. Stir by hand to combine.

3. Place egg, buttermilk and oil into the Vitamix container and secure lid.

4. Select Variable 2.

5. Switch machine to Start and blend for 15 seconds.

6. Pour wet mixture into dry mixture and mix by hand to combine.

7. Pour batter into prepared loaf pan. Sprinkle with 1 teaspoon each of flaxseed, sesame seed and sunflower seeds.

8. Bake for 50 to 55 minutes or until a knife inserted in the center comes out clean. Cool in pan for 10 minutes. Remove from pan and cool completely.

9. Toast in a dry skillet over medium high heat until lightly browned. Toss pan frequently to prevent from burning. Let cool 10 minutes.

nutritional information: *Amount Per Slice: Calories 200, Total Fat 9g, Saturated Fat 1g, Cholesterol 15mg, Sodium 230mg, Total Carbohydrate 25g Dietary Fiber 2g, Protein 5g*

whole grain zucchini *bread*

preparation: 15 minutes • *processing:* 25 seconds plus Pulsing • *bake time:* 1 hour 10 minutes
yield: 1 loaf (16 slices)

1 1/2 cups (300 g) granulated sugar,
divided use

2 1/4 teaspoons ground cinnamon,
divided use

2 1/2 cups (312 g) all-purpose flour

1 cup (80 g) rolled oats

1 teaspoon baking powder

3/4 teaspoon salt

1/2 teaspoon baking soda

3 large eggs

1/2 cup (122 g) unsweetened applesauce

1 teaspoon vanilla extract

1/4 cup (56 g) unsalted butter

10 ounces (284 g) zucchini, cut into
large chunks

1 cup (120 g) chopped walnuts or pecans

3/4 cup (120 g) raisins

1. Preheat oven to 350°F (180°C). Spray a 9–inch x 5–inch (23 cm x 13 cm) loaf pan with cooking spray.

2. Combine 1 Tablespoon of sugar and 1/4 teaspoon of cinnamon and set aside.

3. Place flour, oats, baking powder, salt, baking soda and remaining cinnamon in a large-size mixing bowl and stir by hand to combine.

4. Place zucchini into the Vitamix container and secure lid.

5. Select Variable 4.

6. Pulse 3 times. Stop and scrape down sides with a spatula. Repeat this process 2 more times. Place zucchini in a strainer to drain out extra moisture.

7. Place eggs, remaining sugar, applesauce, vanilla and butter into the Vitamix container in the order listed and secure lid.

8. Select Variable 1.

9. Switch machine to Start and slowly increase speed to Variable 5.

10. Blend for 15 seconds. Stop and scrapes down sides with a spatula. Reduce speed to Variable 2. Switch machine to Start and blend for 10 seconds.

11. Pour wet mixture into dry mixture and mix by had to combine. Fold in chopped zucchini, nuts and raisins. Spoon into prepared pan and sprinkle with cinnamon-sugar mixture.

12. Bake for 1 hour 10 minutes or until toothpick inserted in center comes out clean. Cool in pan on wire rack for 10 minutes. Remove from pan and cool completely on wire rack.

chopping nuts

To chop nuts in your Vitamix machine, place them in the container and secure the lid. Select Variable 4. Pulse 4 times or until desired chop is reached. For best results, chop 2 cups (295 g) at a time, and store leftovers at room temperature in an airtight container.

nutritional information: *Amount Per Slice: Calories 280, Total Fat 9g, Saturated Fat 2.5g, Cholesterol 45mg, Sodium 200mg, Total Carbohydrate 46g, Dietary Fiber 2g, Protein 5g*

overnight chocolate *coffee cake*

preparation: 20 minutes plus refrigeration • **processing:** Pulsing plus 15 seconds
bake time: 60–65 minutes • **yield:** 8 servings

1 1/3 cups (167 g) all-purpose flour, divided use

1 1/3 cups (160 g) whole wheat flour, divided use

2/3 cup (53 g) rolled oats

1/2 cup (110 g) lightly packed brown sugar

1/2 teaspoon ground cinnamon

1/2 cup plus 1/3 cup (182 g) unsalted butter, divided use

1 cup (224 g) semi-sweet chocolate pieces

1 1/2 teaspoons baking powder

1/4 teaspoon baking soda

1/4 teaspoon salt

2 large eggs

1 cup (245 g) nonfat plain yogurt

2/3 cup (133 g) granulated sugar

1. Grease a 9–inch (23 cm) deep dish pie plate.

2. To make the topping, place 1/3 cup (42 g) all-purpose flour, 1/3 cup (40 g) whole wheat flour, oats, brown sugar, cinnamon and 1/3 cup (70 g) butter into the Vitamix container in the order listed and secure lid.

3. Select Variable 4.

4. Pulse 6 times. Pour into a bowl and stir in chocolate pieces. Set aside.

5. Place 1 cup (125 g) all-purpose flour, 1 cup (120 g) whole wheat flour, baking powder, baking soda and salt in a medium-sized mixing bowl and mix by hand to combine.

6. Place eggs, yogurt, 1/2 cup (112 g) butter and sugar into the Vitamix container in the order listed and secure lid.

7. Select Variable 4.

8. Switch machine to Start and blend for 15 seconds.

9. Pour wet mixture into dry mixture and stir by hand to combine.

10. Spread the batter into the pie plate. Sprinkle with half of the topping. Spread on the remaining batter and top with remaining topping. Cover and refrigerate 4 to 24 hours.

11. Preheat oven to 350°F (180°C). Uncover coffee cake. Tent with foil to prevent burning and bake for 30 minutes. Uncover and bake an additional 25 to 35 minutes or until toothpick inserted in center comes out clean.

 **nutritional information:** *Amount Per Serving: Calories 600, Total Fat 30g, Saturated Fat 17g, Cholesterol 100mg, Sodium 230mg, Total Carbohydrate 81g, Dietary Fiber 4g, Protein 9g*

tasteful pairings

This delicious coffee cake can pull double duty. Pair with the Burst of Berries Smoothie (Beverages) for a quick morning meal, or with the Creamy Butter Frosting (Desserts) for a mouth-watering dessert.

holiday *hot cakes*
with sweet raspberry *topping*

preparation: 20 minutes • ***processing:*** 1 minute 15 seconds • ***cook time:*** 15 – 20 minutes
yield: 2 1/3 cups (560 ml) syrup, 16 pancakes

4 cups (454 g) frozen unsweetened raspberries, divided use

1/2 cup (120 ml) water

1/2 cup (120 ml) honey

1 cup (125 g) all-purpose flour

1 cup (120 g) whole wheat flour

1 1/2 teaspoons baking powder

1/2 teaspoon baking soda

1/2 teaspoon ground cinnamon

1/2 teaspoon ground ginger

1/4 teaspoon salt

3 large eggs

1/3 cup (80 ml) honey

1 1/2 cups (360 ml) 2% milk

1 cup (240 g) canned pumpkin

1/2 teaspoon vanilla extract

1. Place 3 cups (340 g) raspberries and water in a saucepan. Bring to a boil, cover, and cook 5 minutes. Let cool 10 minutes.

2. Place mixture into the Vitamix container, add honey and secure lid.

3. Select Variable 1.

4. Switch machine to Start and slowly increase speed to Variable 10.

5. Blend for 45 seconds. Pour back into sauce pan and add remaining berries. Keep warm until serving.

6. Combine flours, baking powder, baking soda, cinnamon, ginger and salt by hand in a large-size mixing bowl.

7. Place eggs, 1/3 cup (80 ml) honey, milk, pumpkin, and vanilla into the Vitamix container in the order listed and secure lid.

8. Select Variable 1.

9. Switch machine to Start and slowly increase speed to Variable 4. Blend for 15 seconds.

10. Heat a nonstick griddle over medium high heat. Ladle 1/3 cup onto skillet for each pancake. Cook 2 minutes each side.

11. Serve with syrup and dust with powdered sugar.

>> **nutritional information:** *Amount Per 4 Pancakes with 1/4 Cup (60 g) Topping: Calories 480, Total Fat 7g, Saturated Fat 2.5g, Cholesterol 145mg, Sodium 590mg, Total Carbohydrate 94g, Dietary Fiber 8g, Protein 16g*

create your own breakfast *bread*

preparation: 20 minutes • **processing:** Pulsing • **bake time:** 55–60 minutes
yield: 1 loaf (12 slices)

choose your fruit or vegetable:

2 medium apples, cored, quartered

1 medium firm pear, cored, quartered

1 medium zucchini, quartered

2 medium carrots, halved

choose your mix-ins to equal 1 3/4 cups:

(limit to 3/4 cup) walnuts, dried apricots or dried cherries

(limit to 3/4 cup) pecans, rolled oats or pitted dates

raisins or semisweet chocolate chips

(limit to 3/4 cup) almonds or sweetened shredded coconut

common ingredients:

1 1/4 cups (156 g) all-purpose flour

1 teaspoon baking powder

1 teaspoon salt

1/2 teaspoon baking soda

1/2 teaspoon ground cinnamon

1/2 teaspoon ground nutmeg

2 large eggs

1/2 cup (120 ml) light olive oil

1/2 cup (120 g) plain yogurt

1 teaspoon vanilla extract

1 teaspoon orange zest

3/4 cup (150 g) granulated sugar

1. Preheat oven to 350°F (180°C). Lightly grease a 9-inch x 5-inch (23 cm x 13 cm) loaf pan.

2. If choosing apple or pear, place into the Vitamix container, fill with 3 cups (720 ml) water and secure lid.

3. Select Variable 7.

4. Pulse 8 to 10 times or until chopped. Drain well. Measure out 1 cup.

5. If choosing zucchini or carrot, place quartered sections into the Vitamix container and secure lid.

6. Select Variable 7.

7. Pulse 8 to 10 times until chopped. Measure out 1 cup.

8. Choose your mix-ins. Measure and place in small bowl.

9. Place flour, baking powder, salt, baking soda, cinnamon and nutmeg into a medium-sized mixing bowl and mix by hand to combine. Stir in your choice of mix-ins.

10. Place 1 cup (150 g) fruit or vegetable, eggs, oil, yogurt, orange zest and sugar into the Vitamix container and secure lid.

11. Select Variable 1.

12. Switch machine to Start and slowly increase speed to Variable 5.

13. Blend for 15 seconds.

14. Pour wet mixture into dry mixture and mix by hand to combine.

15. Pour into prepared loaf pan and bake for 55 to 60 minutes or until toothpick inserted into center comes out clean. Cool in pan on wire rack for 30 minutes. Remove from pan and cool completely.

 nutritional information: *Amount Per Slice (with apple, walnuts, oats and raisins): Calories 210, Total Fat 12g, Saturated Fat 1.5g, Cholesterol 25mg, Sodium 230mg, Total Carbohydrate 25g, Dietary Fiber 1g, Protein 3g*

apple *pancakes*

preparation: 15 minutes • ***processing:*** 20 seconds • ***yield:*** 26 pancakes (13 servings)

2 cups (240 g) whole wheat flour

2 Tablespoons (30 g) baking powder

1 teaspoon baking soda

1 teaspoon salt

6 Tablespoons (75 g) granulated sugar

1/2 teaspoon ground nutmeg

2 cups (480 ml) milk

2 large eggs

1 Tablespoon butter

1/2 teaspoon vanilla extract

1 medium apple, 5 ounces (142 g), cored, quartered

1. Combine flour, baking powder, baking soda, salt, sugar and nutmeg in a medium-sized mixing bowl by hand. Set aside.

2. Place milk, eggs, butter, vanilla and apple into the Vitamix container in the order listed and secure lid.

3. Select Variable 1.

4. Switch machine to Start and slowly increase speed to Variable 5.

5. Blend for 20 seconds.

6. Pour wet mixture into dry mixture and mix by hand until combined.

7. Let batter sit for 5 to 10 minutes before cooking to yield best texture and flavor.

 nutritional information: *Amount Per 2 Pancake Serving: Calories 130, Total Fat 3.5g Saturated Fat 1.5g, Cholesterol 35mg, Sodium 540mg, Total Carbohydrate 23g, Dietary Fiber 2g, Protein 5g*

apple picking

It's fun to experiment with different apple varieties that are in season to change up the flavor of this recipe. Some apples are becoming more scarce on supermarket shelves, so it's fun to see what you can find at your local farmer's market. Braeburn apples are sweet, juicy, and crisp, and are available from fall through mid-summer. Fuji apples, available year round, are extra-sweet and hold their texture during baking.

note: Use 3/4 cup (150 g) of wheat berries in place of whole wheat flower. Grind berries into flour using a Vitamix Dry Blade container for 1 minute on High prior to using in recipe.

potato cheddar breakfast *bake*

preparation: 20 minutes • **processing:** 20–25 seconds • **bake time:** 1 hour 20 minutes
yield: 10 servings

1 1/4 pounds (568 g) Russet potatoes, cubed

8 large eggs

2 cups (480 ml) milk

1/2 teaspoon salt

8 ounces (227 g) cheddar cheese, in large cubes

1/4 cup (40 g) chopped green pepper

1/4 cup (40 g) chopped onion

1 1/2 cups (210 g) diced ham

1. Preheat oven to 350°F (180°C). Spray a 9-inch x 9-inch (23 cm x 23 cm) baking pan with cooking spray.

2. Hash potatoes using the wet chop method. Drain and reserve.

3. Place eggs, milk, salt and cheese into the Vitamix container in the order listed and secure lid.

4. Select Variable 1.

5. Switch machine to Start and slowly increase speed to Variable 5.

6. Blend for 10 seconds.

7. Reduce speed to Variable 2 and remove the lid plug.

8. Add peppers, onion, potatoes and ham through the lid plug opening.

9. Blend for 10–15 seconds.

10. Pour into prepared pan. Bake covered for 40 to 45 minutes. Uncover and bake another 30 to 35 minutes until firm and lightly browned.

>> **nutritional information:** *Amount Per Serving: Calories 270, Total Fat 15g, Saturated Fat 8g, Cholesterol 195mg, Sodium 350mg, Total Carbohydrate 14g, Dietary Fiber 1g, Protein 19g*

oatmeal cranberry *pancakes*

preparation: 15 minutes plus rest time • **processing:** 20 seconds
yield: 10 pancakes

1 1/2 cups (360 ml) milk

1 large egg

1 cup (120 g) whole wheat flour

2 teaspoons baking powder

1/2 teaspoon baking soda

1/2 teaspoon salt

1/4 cup (40 g) flax seed meal

3/4 cup (115 g) rolled oats

1/4 cup (30 g) dried cranberries

2 Tablespoons (20 g) unsalted sunflower seeds

1. Place milk, egg, flour, baking powder, baking soda, salt and flax seed meal into the Vitamix container in the order listed and secure lid.

2. Select Variable 1.

3. Switch machine to Start and slowly increase speed to Variable 10.

4. Blend for 10 seconds. Stop machine and remove lid.

5. Add oats, cranberries and sunflower seeds into the Vitamix container and secure lid.

6. Select Variable 2.

7. Switch machine to Start and blend for 10 seconds, using the tamper if necessary to press the ingredients into the blades.

8. Let batter sit for 5 to 10 minutes before cooking to yield best texture and flavor.

 **nutritional information:** *Amount Per Pancake: Calories 120, Total Fat 4g, Saturated Fat 1g, Cholesterol 20mg, Sodium 180mg, Total Carbohydrate 18g, Dietary Fiber 3g, Protein 5g*

oven baked onion cheese *frittata*

preparation: 20 minutes • **processing:** 15 seconds • **bake time:** 20–25 minutes
yield: 8 servings

1/4 cup (40 g) chopped onion

1 cup (115 g) diced summer squash

1/4 cup (40 g) diced red bell pepper

1/4 cup (40 g) diced green bell pepper

2 Tablespoons (30 ml) olive oil

6 large eggs

1/2 cup (50 g) grated Parmesan cheese

1/2 teaspoon dried oregano

1/8 teaspoon ground nutmeg

1/2 teaspoon salt

1/4 teaspoon ground black pepper

1/2 cup (65 g) cubed cheddar cheese

1. Preheat oven to 350°F (180°C). Spray a 9-inch (23 cm) pie pan with cooking spray.

2. Sauté onion, squash, and peppers in olive oil until soft. Place in bottom of prepared pie pan.

3. Place eggs, Parmesan, oregano, nutmeg, salt and pepper into the Vitamix container in the order listed and secure lid.

4. Select Variable 1.

5. Switch machine to Start and slowly increase speed to Variable 4.

6. Blend for 10 seconds.

7. Remove lid plug. Add cheese through the lid plug opening and blend an additional 5 seconds.

8. Pour mixture over vegetables. Bake 20 to 25 minutes or until set.

 nutritional information: *Amount Per Serving: Calories 150, Total Fat 11g, Saturated Fat 4.5g, Cholesterol 150mg, Sodium 330mg, Total Carbohydrate 2g, Dietary Fiber 0g, Protein 9g*

brunch buffet

A buffet can be a real lifesaver when entertaining a large group. For simpler self-serving and lovely presentation, create individual frittatas for your guests. Place about a tablespoon of the vegetable mixture in each cup of a paper-lined muffin tin, then fill with blended egg mixture. Individual frittatas also make delicious hors d'oeuvres for a baby or bridal shower. With all the different paper muffin cups available, you can coordinate them to match the colors of the event for an extra special touch.

savory brunch *crêpes*

preparation: 15 minutes • **processing:** Pulsing • **cook time:** 10 minutes • **yield:** 6 crêpes

3 cups (290 g) whole mushrooms

4 ounces (114 g) shallot

5 ounces (140 g) baby spinach

1 Tablespoon olive oil

1 teaspoon chopped fresh rosemary

1/2 teaspoon salt

6 Tablespoons (102 g) goat cheese

6 Whole Wheat Crêpes (recipe found in this section)

1. Place mushrooms and shallots into the Vitamix container and secure lid.

2. Select Variable 4.

3. Pulse 5 times. Scrape down sides with a spatula and Pulse 5 more times. Repeat this process until all of the mushrooms are chopped. Empty into a bowl.

4. Place spinach into the Vitamix container and secure lid.

5. Select Variable 4.

6. Pulse 5 times using the tamper. Scrape down sides with a spatula and Pulse 5 more times. Repeat this process until all of the spinach is chopped.

7. Heat olive oil in a large nonstick skillet over medium heat. Add mushrooms, shallot, rosemary and slat. Cook, stirring until the mushrooms are soft, about 5 minutes. Stir in chopped spinach a handful at a time; cook until wilted, about 4 minutes.

8. Place crêpe on a clean cutting board or plate. Spread filling in the center, leaving a 1 to 2-inch (2.5 cm–5 cm) border. Top with a Tablespoon of goat cheese. Fold the right side just past the middle and do the same with the left side. Garnish with fresh chopped rosemary. Repeat with 5 more crêpes.

nutritional information: *Amount Per Crêpe: Calories 210, Total Fat 10g, Saturated Fat 4g, Cholesterol 90mg, Sodium 420mg, Total Carbohydrate 22g, Dietary Fiber 2g, Protein 10g*